EARLY ENDORSEMENTS

I really enjoyed Homeless to Billionaire. *It's a valuable work on wealth creation that also reads like a thrilling adventure story. Take the time to visit the world of Andres Pira; you'll be richly rewarded for it.*

Gay Hendricks, PhD
Author, *The Big Leap*
Founder, The Hendricks Institute
Psychologist

This book shares an inspiring, miraculous story that's a must-read! It's packed full of golden nuggets and proven wealth principles to help you create your own miracle!

Debbie Allen
Author, *The Highly Paid Expert; Success Is EASY*
International speaker

Reading this book is like joining a luxury gym for prosperity. Imagine entering one book and finding all the equipment you need to strengthen every financial muscle in you. Joe and Andres have done that with this book. It's filled with common sense wisdom and inspiration to achieve success in all areas of your life. If you're ready to take your success to the next level, this book is a must-read."

Ike Allen
Spiritual director, Enlightenment Village

I started reading this book only to discover I was hooked in the first few chapters. I've read and written books on how to achieve success but this one had an element that I haven't seen before. Imagine turning from a homeless derelict to a billionaire in an adventure that few could imagine. From a teenage alcoholic to a rising star helping others through generosity and outstandingly good advice—all learned from failure and an accelerated learning experience. I strongly recommend this book if you want to learn eighteen valuable techniques that theoretically could end up making you millions.

Joseph Sugarman

Chairman, BluBlocker Corporation

People who want proof that your mind can create reality need to read this inspiring book. Young Andres went from homeless to billionaire. His eighteen principles are brilliant. They work!

Bob Proctor

International best-selling author

Law of Attraction Coach

Andres's rags-to-riches story clearly demonstrates that anything is possible. Homeless to Billionaire *is packed with powerful principles to be a positive force for good in the world. It's a quick and easy read that will give you an injection of inspiration and practical strategies to succeed at anything you set your mind to.*

Deborah Torres Patel

Author, *Speak Like a Superstar*

International Hall of Fame speaker

This book is a massive dose of inspiration mixed with practical steps for manifesting your big business goals. It's very rare that a book on wealth creation goes so deeply into the abundance mindset and backs it up with science and compelling stories ... and that's what makes it a binge-worthy read. (I couldn't put it down!)

Jeanna Gabellini

Author, *10-Minute Money Makers*

I love it! An inspiring book that works! It will live among the classics!

Christy Whitman

New York Times best-selling author

Founder, QSCA

Certified Law of Attraction Coach

Homeless to Billionaire *is not just a story, but a powerful and authentic roadmap that will lead you out of the dark and into the light. Andres's journey will connect you deeply to those "rock bottom" moments we all experience; it will also give you a sense of great hope and joy with each success. You will be inspired by his immense courage and commitment. But even more than that, Andres is living proof that you, too, can triumph over adversity if you combine a winning, "never give up" attitude with solid principles that really work. If you want to up-level your prosperity or any area of your life, you will not want to be without this detailed "success manual" to guide and inspire you daily.*

Lisa Winston

Author, *Your Turning Point*

Co-host, *The Mindset Reset Show*

HOMELESS TO
BILLIONAIRE

THE 18 PRINCIPLES OF WEALTH ATTRACTION
AND CREATING UNLIMITED OPPORTUNITY

ANDRES PIRA

WITH DR. JOE VITALE

ForbesBooks

Published by ForbesBooks, Charleston, South Carolina.
Member of Advantage Media Group.

ForbesBooks is a registered trademark, and the ForbesBooks colophon is a trademark of Forbes Media, LLC.

Printed in the United States of America.

10   9   8   7   6   5   4   3   2   1

ISBN: 978-1-946633-86-6
LCCN: 2019934675

Cover design by George Stevens.

This publication is designed to provide accurate and authoritative information in regard to the subject matter covered. It is sold with the understanding that the publisher is not engaged in rendering legal, accounting, or other professional services. If legal advice or other expert assistance is required, the services of a competent professional person should be sought.

Advantage Media Group is proud to be a part of the Tree Neutral® program. Tree Neutral offsets the number of trees consumed in the production and printing of this book by taking proactive steps such as planting trees in direct proportion to the number of trees used to print books. To learn more about Tree Neutral, please visit **www.treeneutral.com**.

Since 1917, the Forbes mission has remained constant. Global Champions of Entrepreneurial Capitalism. ForbesBooks exists to further that aim by bringing the Stories, Passion, and Knowledge of top thought leaders to the forefront. ForbesBooks brings you The Best in Business. To be considered for publication, please visit **www.forbesbooks.com**.

To my beloved mother, who passed as I finished this book.
—Andres

TABLE OF CONTENTS

ACKNOWLEDGMENTS

—

Thank you to Dr. Joe Vitale for making this book happen! You are my mentor, my role model, and my friend for life, and I am forever grateful.

With gratitude to Jack Canfield, Brian Tracy, Napoleon Hill, Bob Proctor, and Charles Haanel. You were my first real teachers in life. Through your books I became a lifelong learner.

With gratitude to my sisters and brother: Linda, Kristian, Alejandra, and Annette.

With gratitude to my father for teaching me early in life the skill of discipline. It has served me well.

To my darling daughter, Valentina, for making me want to be a better father and version of myself. You inspired me to guide as many people on this planet into a new awakening and to make you proud of me as your father. It is because of you that I want to be a force for good.

FOREWORD BY JACK CANFIELD

———

I had the pleasure of mentoring Andres for more than sixteen years. The most interesting part of that mentoring process is that I didn't even know I was doing it. Andres had been studying my work for many years, putting my lessons into action, long before I met him. When I finally met Andres, he was already a success. In talking with him, I found out that he had read my work, and the work of other teachers, and had done his best to disprove it (that's correct: *disprove it*). I've worked with millions of people worldwide who generally want to learn the principles I teach. Andres was different. He wanted proof.

A great friend of mine, W. Clement Stone, once said, "Definiteness of purpose is the starting point of all achievement." He couldn't have said it any better. A man is lost without purpose. Lost … without a sense of direction. I was surprised that someone as young as Andres fully understood this quote.

Famed author and radio host Earl Nightingale said that if a ship left the harbor with someone at the controls who had clear directions and a clear sense of purpose, it would get to its destination 99 percent of the time. Without guidance or anyone at the controls, it wouldn't even get out of the harbor. Instinctually, Andres knew this even at his darkest hours. This is wisdom that takes many a lifetime to learn. As a lifelong teacher, I was very much intrigued by Andres's story.

Years ago, I started the Transformational Leadership Council with some of the most powerful transformational leaders, coaches, authors, and filmmakers who, like me, wanted to open the minds and hearts of people everywhere. In my living room, I started a band of teachers, looking for students to transform. Worldwide, we have found ourselves in front of many students, and for that I am eternally grateful. So, imagine my surprise when I met a student who started out trying to disprove my teachings only now to credit me for being a part of his transformation publicly.

For years Andres spent his days like a ship without anyone at the controls. However, when he finally found that purpose and desire, he applied all he learned from reading books like Rhonda Byrne's *The Secret* and then continued to build upon that through ups and downs, successes and failures. Could I have predicted, or could he have foreseen, that as a former gang member he would become one of the most celebrated real estate developers in southern Thailand, a billionaire at the age when most are still trying to decide on their career?

When I read *Homeless to Billionaire* for the first time, it occurred to me that a new generation of transformational leaders was emerging. Leaders who demand proof before they will share knowledge. Proof that the knowledge they learn in books can make a difference when applied outside of the book. When you read Andres's story, you will find yourself saying, "I already knew that, but I never thought to apply it the way he did." *Homeless to Billionaire* is a compilation of the most powerful success principles, mixed with real-life scenarios, that provides the proof that the new generation is looking for when deciding on a leader to follow.

In business, Andres defies logic. Whereas most companies focus on the bottom line, often pinching employee salaries to save money, he believes in paying employees more. While many companies treat employees as workers, Andres treats them as a family with a sincere desire to see them succeed and help them understand how to harness the power of the universe to improve all facets of their own lives. Also, in a time when a generation of millennials demand proof before compliance, Andres has mastered the formula for making his employees believe in the impossible. He knows how to make money, inspire, and drive success like no one I have ever met. When we met for the first time, he credited me—along with others, such as Dr. Joe Vitale and Bob Proctor—with his education and thirst for more.

The book you hold in your hands brings Andres's compelling story and modified success principles to the forefront in a time when it is easier to be skeptical than inspired. *Homeless to Billionaire* teaches about vibrational giving, the power of goal setting, how to think bigger, how to increase profit through employee motivation, and how to control your emotions and eliminate any negatives in your life. His raw, honest story is compelling and laced with specific business practices and challenges to help you face your fears. It captures everything he has learned from personal development gurus and everything he has proven to be real in the world of business. The result is a business book like no other and a personal memoir that makes you take a step back.

When I wrote *Chicken Soup for the Soul,* I had never imagined more than one million people would read my book. My prediction is that when one million people read Andres's book, he won't be surprised because he has learned to expect success. He'll ask for success, believe it will happen, and see it achieved. It's how he started his journey homeless on a beach, expecting success to come to him.

What Andres has taught me, the Chicken Soup guy, is that if the teacher does their job right, it's inevitable that the teacher becomes the student.

—Jack Canfield

Jack Canfield is the coauthor of the *Chicken Soup for the Soul* series and *The Success Principles: How to Get From Where You Are to Where You Want to Be.*

INTRODUCTION
—
THE STORY OF
A MIRACLE

Whatever the mind of a man can conceive, it can achieve.

—**Napoleon Hill**, *Think and Grow Rich*

Does this apply to the secret to riches?

Can you *really* change your life from survival to success by changing your mind?

Is it possible to create your opportunities?

People are always asking me whether *Law of Attraction*, *The Secret*, *Think and Grow Rich*, and other books about success principles *really* work the way they are written.

In short, the answer to all these questions is a resounding yes. This book, *Homeless to Billionaire*, proves it. It's how a man morphs

1

from a life of destitution in a strange land to becoming a billionaire on his own. Not a millionaire. Not a multimillionaire. A billionaire.

I first met Andres Pira in 2017 when I agreed to speak at his first live seminar in Thailand.

Homeless at the age of twenty, sleeping on the beaches of Thailand, starving, frustrated, and angry at his situation, Andres had no idea that in the lowest moment of his life he would find salvation. As fate would have it, someone gave him a copy of the book, *The Secret*.

While his success didn't happen overnight, today he runs nineteen companies, has more than two hundred employees, and is the largest real estate developer in southern Thailand. He continues to apply what he learned in *The Secret* to see more prominent and more significant results. He has only just begun.

Even though I was there to appear at his live event with other guest speakers, I convinced him to go on stage for the first time in his life and share his survival-to-success story.

Then, I convinced him to write down the eighteen principles he used to achieve his success. Next, I asked if I could help him write his story into a book. He agreed.

You are holding this book right now.

At thirty-six, he was almost half my age, but we both had many things in common.

I, too, was once homeless, struggling through poverty for more than ten years. I went from nothing to something, from unpublished to published, to even appearing in a movie, which led to more accomplishments than I can list here.

But I still knew there was much more to learn from him. I wanted to know exactly what he had discovered on his journey from the lonely beaches he lived on when homeless to the incredible luxury beach resorts that he now builds all over the world. I'm pretty sure you want to know what these discoveries are, too.

Andres is an inspiration to us all.

Let me tell you a story that Andres would not tell you himself; it's a lesson in love and gratitude and why you should strive to be wealthy, too.

Early in 2018, Andres's mother became terminally ill. His mother sacrificed for Andres her entire life, and ultimately was the person who freed Andres's tortured soul by permitting him to fail. Learning that she was ill, Andres dropped everything to be with her. Flying her from Sweden to Bangkok, he secured the best medical care and made sure to surround her with people whom she loved.

Her illness was aggressive and doctors warned that she had very little time left to live. She made two dying requests. First, she wanted the family together. The second request was that she wanted to die in Sweden, the country that became her home for many years.

Andres instantly started making phone calls. He hired a private jet. Andres retained a life support team of doctors and nurses to fly with her and some to stay with her in Sweden. He spared no expense to honor his mother's last requests, even bringing his sisters and brother from Sweden to Thailand to be by her bedside. As a family, they spent four weeks, every day, with their mom. He then flew her to Sweden where she died as she had asked.

When you read his story, you will understand why this was something that Andres had to do for his mother. His ability to provide for her, in the end, was a significant experience honoring his mother's impact on his life. What I took from this story that made me cry when he told it to me was that love and gratitude are freeing. Being able to give these gifts to his mother was priceless. The ability for him to pull such extraordinary measures to make this happen, of course, came from his wealth. The story of his mother is an example of how money is neutral, not good or bad. It is how you choose to use it that makes all the difference. Wealth affords the option to do the extraordinary. I encourage you to learn from his wealth attraction principles.

As you read this book, keep in mind what I genuinely believe and like to say: "Expect miracles."

—Dr. Joe Vitale

Dr. Joe Vitale is a contributor to *The Secret.*

PROVE ME WRONG!

—

You have probably already heard the wealth principles I'm about to outline. You'll read them and think to yourself, "Oh, I know this." Or perhaps you've never read about these principles before, and you'll dismiss them as common sense. Both are fine reactions. I learned the hard way that knowledge is not what gets us what we want in life—it is putting that knowledge into action.

You're about to learn how to put eighteen principles into practice with clarity and ease to unlock your full potential and obtain the accomplishments you desire.

These principles for attracting wealth took me years to thoroughly learn. As you'll read, I didn't start life as a billionaire. I was lucky to see my eighteenth birthday. At one of my lowest points, I discovered the power of knowledge through a book. By studying, learning, and putting into action the knowledge I've acquired from many books, I turned my "survival lifestyle" into one of abundance and possibility. The results I experienced were nothing short of amazing. I was humbled. I am grateful.

Maybe you're a skeptic when it comes to the Law of Attraction and manifestation, especially in business. After all, millions worldwide have read motivational books, and not everyone has been able to see results as I have. The difference lies in taking a specific *action*.

You are reading a business book crafted from the journey of self-discovery. The principles I used for wealth attraction and creating unlimited opportunity in my business were inspired by the massive change I experienced using them in my personal life. The reason my story resonates with people all over the world, as well as world-class speakers like Dr. Joe Vitale, is that these principles are not theory, they are the result of years of study, trial and error, and being disciplined enough to be open to the results. As a successful businessman, I can tell you that applying these principles to your business will generate results, and I hope that sharing them through my personal story will show you how they can be highly effective in your own life as well.

> *Your past cannot be altered. The future is yours to shape in any way you imagine.*

Many of the teachings in this book were learned from books and mentors. Most have been documented for centuries and many in recent clinical research studies. Others I discovered while developing my companies over the years. I've combined them into the eighteen principles that I now have seen proven over and over again through action and results. They are a combination of twenty-plus years of my thirst for knowledge and understanding mined from seminars I've attended to one-on-one conversations I've been privileged to have with some of the world's top success experts.

What I have done is modify this knowledge to fit into my modern-day life and business. I've distilled the information and added to it. Most importantly, I have lived what I teach.

I've distilled it to eighteen principles. Each is designed to create opportunity and attract abundant wealth. It might be a little awkward at first, but trust and be patient. You'll quickly come to realize how easy each of the principles is to apply. Don't become overwhelmed by trying to put all eighteen into action right away. As you read, it will become clear which ones you can implement right away while others may take longer to incorporate. Each principle has a unique value.

I've spent a decade with some of the most successful people in the world who implement these same principles. Now, it's your turn. In the end, you may discount it all. I welcome your correspondence on such claims. I will laugh because that's what I thought when I first began my journey. Trying to debunk that knowledge led me to live a life most only dream about. I challenge you! Go ahead, prove my eighteen principles wrong. I can't wait to hear how they have changed your life forever too.

Most people dream of great achievements; very few wake up and fulfill them.

PRINCIPLE #1

—

LEAD A LASER-FOCUSED LIFE

I can be whatever I will to be.

—Charles F. Haanel, *The New Master Key System*

WE ALL COME FROM SOMEWHERE

I grew up very confident that I would never become someone whom my parents could be proud to call "son." This one, unjustified, negative thought almost got me killed before my eighteenth birthday and led me to destitution.

I was born on a tiny Colombian island in the Caribbean Sea named San Andres, thus the origin of my name. My father had left his home country of Sweden fairly young and opened a restaurant on this island surrounded by beautiful blue waters. It was here that he met my mother. At the time the island wasn't a safe place. My father carried a revolver wherever he went. Also, my parents grappled with wanting their children to have a Swedish education. These two things—the lack of safety and the desire for a better education for their children— were the reasons my parents made the huge sacrifice to move back to Sweden when my mother became pregnant with my sister.

I was three when my family moved, and just four years later my parents divorced. They never told me why, but I could hear glass and ornaments smashing outside my bedroom door while I cried, holding my ears and praying for it to stop. It was enough to know that things were not well between them. Thinking back on my childhood, I only have fragmented memories and very few details of the places where my life began.

> *Sometimes a darker past needs to stay in the past so you can move forward and create a brighter future.*

My father was strict, requiring me to do my homework immediately after school. Every night, when I emerged from my room, he would take one of my schoolbooks and ask me questions to make sure I had done my homework correctly. He wanted proof that I knew the information I needed to pass my tests. One wrong answer and I was sent back to my room until I mastered every part of my homework for that evening. While there were nights I resented my father's harsh and strict methods, I learned valuable skills that would come into play later in life. I owe my sense of dedication and discipline when it comes to studying and gaining knowledge to my father.

My mother's lessons, the ones that would shape my life, were the ones you couldn't learn in school. She would teach them to me after I left home.

Though my parents were divorced, they lived close to each other. I saw them both regularly, and if by chance I had a falling out with one, I could stay with the other. I spent countless nights drifting between their two homes and somewhere between them, trying to figure out where I belonged.

As a child, I would feel consumed by the thought that I had no control over my day-by-day existence. So, in the space between my parents' homes, I forged behaviors unbecoming of someone on his way to a successful life.

LIVING WITHOUT FOCUS

My status as the "tough boy" was more important than the reputation of being the "clever boy." Though I knew the answers to my teachers' questions, I never raised my hand. It was part of the façade I had created. I was often disciplined for bad behavior in school.

The famous German philosopher Arthur Schopenhauer once said, "The two enemies of human happiness are pain and boredom." He was right about boredom. Boredom, along with an impulsive mindset, didn't make for smart decisions. I earned reprimands for stunts like placing *real* Swedish fish (not the candy) in the air duct at school, causing a foul odor that shut the school down for three days.

Why was I focused on putting a value on the things that would hurt me? Why was being destructive so desirable?

The simple answer was that I was living a life without focus, without knowing what I wanted to do, be, or have in life. I walked through life not connecting my choices to my outcomes.

CHOICES DICTATE OUTCOMES

At fifteen, I dropped out of high school, and I became addicted to the party-hard lifestyle. When you have no goals and a strong need to feel things happen to you—good or bad—the party always finds you. My life was one big party.

Seldom did a day go by when I was not drinking on the streets of Stockholm while most kids my age were in school. I became very skilled at pushing through the day with a foggy alcohol brain.

My gang of friends shared my limited ambitions, making hanging out on the streets easy. Soon groups of friends partying together turned into gangs of friends fighting, sometimes with each other, often with other gangs. There was one rule of the suburban streets of Stockholm—never show weakness or fear. I earned my street cred by landing punches and never showing pain, no matter how shattered my knuckles felt from hitting bones.

THE VOICE YOU HEAR AT ROCK BOTTOM

Continuous intoxication dulls the senses. From my teenage years, I remember three things: avoiding, drinking, and justifying. As I've said, I did not have the confidence that I could amount to anything my parents would be proud of, so I lived without specific goals. I felt as if I had already failed, so why work to achieve anything? I was, by default, on my way to becoming a lifelong alcoholic, a mistake or two away from prison or, worse, a grave. I was no stranger to being arrested, picking fights, overindulging, or creating trouble for no reason at all. At eighteen, I wondered if I would see my nineteenth birthday.

THE DAY I THOUGHT I WOKE UP DEAD

As I grew older and physically stronger, so did my rage.

The street fights and bar brawls became more frequent and intense. The first turning point in my life was waking up on the steps of an abandoned building, head pounding, clothes filthy, and with no idea where I was or how I had gotten there, wondering aloud, "I am dead? Did I die?"

A whole day passed with me on those steps. My body felt disconnected from my head. I lay in broken glass. I couldn't shake the thought that I woke up dead and was sitting on the steps of the deceased.

When I returned home, the look on my mother's face was indescribable. Without her saying one word, I felt her hurt, worry, disappointment, desperation, and anger flow through me. It hurt worse than any punch I'd ever received.

When my father heard I had returned, he and my mother argued over "what to do with Andres." I was immediately transported back to my old room again, a young child, tears flowing and hands over my ears.

I was at a crossroad. I began to fear my mother would feel responsible if something was to happen to me, that in some way she might believe she had supported her son's partying ways that got him killed. On the other hand, I did not want to live by my father's rules. Most importantly, I no longer wanted to be the center of their arguments. I had to start taking responsibility for myself. So, I decided to get my first job. At rock bottom, this felt like a monumental decision.

KNOWING WHEN TO START OVER

The very first job I got in Sweden was for a telemarketing office selling prepaid SIM cards, making two hundred to three hundred calls for eight hours every day. I hated my job. I was in constant darkness—metaphorically in my mind, but literally in my waking world, as my working hours were from noon to nine in the evening. When I finished work it would already be dark and cold outside. I hated everything about this job. I had also committed to going out to party only on the weekends, so I had minimal contact with people during the week. To hold down a job during the week, not party or drink or fight, I had to separate from the friends I had hung out with during our "gang time." I became isolated, with no social life outside my working hours.

My new responsible lifestyle brought me to a state of depression that I never thought possible. I lacked any motivation, so I was willing to stay in a job that made me depressed. I had to separate from friends and partying to stay the course, but I was alone and isolated.

Worse, the situation created a space in my mind that harbored resentment, frustration, self-pity, and anger. My thoughts were always wrapped up in these emotions.

I found any excuse not to go to work, leading to my dismissal. I immediately blamed it on the company, my managers, and the customers. The outcome was not my fault, I told myself. It's what we all tell ourselves when we won't take responsibility.

I believed that if you did not have an excellent education, you would never be able to get a good job. So, I felt stuck.

My doctor prescribed three different antidepressants. Happy to escape my day-to-day, I took the medications, which made things worse. I became completely isolated from the world, so paranoid that someone was coming for me that I stood by my front door, often for hours, waiting for "them" to arrive. It was a complete mental breakdown.

In the darkness, at my lowest point, I heard a voice say, "You are better than this." The voice I was hearing became persistent.

The voice, which I now know is the universe, was trying to tell me something. I was not ready to hear it. I could hear the voice say, "You are better than this," but I didn't know what to do with this information. So, as it often does, the universe changed tactics.

The same year, my grandfather passed away. Just like that, without warning. The impact hit like a ton of bricks. His death put a blaring thought in my head: "*I will never be better than this unless I escape from here.*"

I knew I had to leave this all behind if I wanted any chance of survival. I knew deep down in my gut that I had to disappear and find what I truly wanted in life. I needed distance from it all to gain a new perspective.

Two months later, the universe came knocking again. My grandfather had left my sister, Linda, my brother, Kristian, and me $2,000 each. When my father handed me the check, he specifically told me to save it for an education or put it in a savings account for later years. Holding the $2,000 in my hand I had an inspired thought. I could use this money to fly away—buy a ticket and vanish. I could force myself to start over.

I had no idea where the one-way ticket would take me, or what I would do when I got there, or how I would survive without knowing anyone. I pushed any hesitation out of my head. The voice I heard now said, "Don't worry about the 'how.'"

START WITH A GOAL

Knowing *exactly* what you want in life is the first principle of wealth attraction. You must decide on specific goals that you want to achieve and be very clear about those goals and their importance in your life. The key is to keep that goal in the forefront of your mind and be open to adjusting it as new opportunities arise. Did I understand this when I bought that plane ticket? Absolutely not! I'm grateful that the universe understood it for me.

What I did understand was that I had to become laser-focused on exactly what I wanted to do, be, and have.

THE SUCCESS DIFFERENCE

I have studied success masters like Jack Canfield, Dr. Joe Vitale, Brian Tracy, Napoleon Hill, and others, reading their books and attending their seminars. I have found that these successful leaders share a trait with some of the wealthiest people in the world: writing down their goals. The research supports it, the masters preach it, and my own experience has proven it to me. Writing down goals is nonnegotiable. Each year I write down 101 goals that I will achieve in the next twelve months. It works! I make it a big part of running my companies.

I am a high school dropout and former gang member who did not have the support of a wealthy family. I've been homeless, bankrupt, and clinically depressed. I have achieved incredible success despite these limitations. I am virtually no different from anyone else. The laser focus I have on my goals and the discipline I apply to them allows me to attract wealth and unlimited opportunity in my life. Goal setting is powerful.

APPLYING GOAL SETTING TO BUSINESS

Most people, when asked about their goals, are not sure of their goals or cannot articulate them in a clearly defined manner. Part of my success in business has come from teaching my employees how to dream and identify their goals through a goal-setting exercise:

1. Write down all the things you don't want in life.

2. Once you have nothing left to write, draw a line after the last thing you don't want in life.

3. Then, on a new sheet of paper, write the opposite of what you just wrote. For example, if you wrote, "I don't want to be poor," then on your new sheet of paper write, "I want to be rich." If you wrote, "I don't want to be alone," then write the opposite, "I want to be in a relationship." And so on: I don't want to be sick—I want to be healthy. I don't want to be stuck here forever—I want to travel and see new things.

4. Once you have completed your opposite list, make a third list: "What can I start doing today?" This list is meant to bring specifics to each thing you do want in life. For example, "What can I do today that I enjoy and will make me wealthy?" Alternatively, "If I don't want to be lonely, what kind of activities, work, and hobbies could I do today that would allow me to have a great social presence and love life?" Or, "If I want to be healthy, what sports or exercises would I enjoy that will impact my health positively?"

5. Once you have created the "What Can I Do Today?" list, circle the top five sentences that inspire you the most and add a reasonable timeline to take action toward these goals.

Then, circle the next five and so on until everything is circled with deadlines.

6.   Keep your final list accessible so that as you begin to take action, you can adjust your list's details and timelines.

7.   Thinking about what you don't want and about changing that into what you do want creates a foundation for building goals with real intent and action. It also trains you to live in positivity. This is more than positive thinking. Science supports goal setting.

EMPLOYEES WHO SET GOALS PERFORM BETTER

Sitting with employees to discuss their goals has a substantial impact on·results, both from a motivational perspective and from a performance perspective. One of my top agents started in our organization six years ago with no real goals or desires in life. He was eager to learn and adapted well to the lessons I offered. He ended up writing ninety-two goals that he wanted to accomplish and put into action. With this proven strategy, he had accomplished eighty-three of ninety-two goals in less than six years.

THE ANATOMY OF WEALTH ATTRACTION

There is a connection between what we visualize in our minds and what we bring into reality with our physical actions. Through visualization, we can alter the strength of our brainwaves to help us connect what we desire and our physical ability to achieve it. I call this the Anatomy of Wealth Attraction.

STUDY: PLAYING THE PIANO IN YOUR MIND[1]

Research from Harvard University focused on the brain and how thoughts affect it by having two groups play piano—one in reality and the other in their mind. Both groups had the same intellect, and neither had been trained to play the piano. One group was told to play scales every day on the piano. The other group was to play by merely thinking about playing the same piano scales as group one.

Scans were done before the study to measure brain activity. After the study, both groups had their brains scanned a second time. The scans measured any structural changes as a result of the piano playing, both imaginary and real.

In both groups, the part of the brain corresponding with finger movements (from piano playing) showed considerable growth. This demonstrated that just thinking about playing the piano had the power to change the brain as if they had physically been playing the scales all along.

Shaping your reality requires visualizing your future in full-color detail.

"FULL-COLOR" DETAILED GOALS

Don't be vague when stating your goals, such as saying, "I want to be rich," or "I want to be healthy." Those are just the first sentences in the paragraph detailing your goals. When you set a new goal, always ask and answer these three questions:

---

1   A. Pascual-Leone, D. Nguyet, LG. Cohen, J.P. Brasil-Neto, A. Cammarota, M. Hallett, "Modulation of muscle responses evoked by transcranial magnetic stimulation during the acquisition of new fine motor skills,"*Journal of Neurophysiology* 74, no. 3, September 1995: 1037-45. doi: 10.1152/jn.1995.74.3.1037.

1. How will that item or experience look in detail when I receive it?

2. How long do I give myself until I reach it?

3. How will I feel and act when I achieve it?

An example might be: *I want to be wealthy*—I want to earn an extra $50,000 this year and I want to make it within the next four months at the latest. I will feel relief, happiness, joy, and peace to have that extra income and be able to take care of my family and my debt.

Bright, vivid mental pictures are essential to creating opportunity in your life. You don't need to understand the *how* of reaching your goals, just be clear on exactly what you want and how you will feel when you reach them.

PRINCIPLE #2

—

TAKE RISKS, RESPONSIBILITY, AND ACTION

He who is not courageous enough to take risks will accomplish nothing in life.

—Muhammad Ali

How do you tell your parents you're leaving and don't know if you are ever coming back?

I was overcome with nervousness, but I had finally gained the strength to go after what I wanted in life. I was about to face my parents and tell them that I just needed to start over. I had to do something before the negativity in my life took hold of me again.

As the three of us gathered at my mother's house, I stared at the floor, gathering my thoughts, swallowing lumps of air. Minutes passed. One idea stayed solid in my mind: *You can't go backward.*

Then, as if someone else was saying it, the words tumbled out in the most ungraceful way:

"I'm leaving. I've decided to leave. Not just for a while. Forever. I can't stand it here anymore. I'm stuck. My life. I'm stuck in my own life." I couldn't stop the words from tumbling out. "I need ... I need someplace else in the world to be happy."

I was painfully aware that my words crippled my mother. She had worked tirelessly to give me a happy life. My father questioned my sanity and then moved to rationalize.

I pulled the ticket out of my back pocket. "I already used the money from Grandfather. I bought the ticket."

My mother, silent the whole time, finally turned toward me. The look in her eyes made me weak. How could I leave her, maybe forever? My hands began to shake again. I was trying to find a response so that I could take that look out of her eyes, but I didn't have to, for she spoke first.

"Andres, go. Go. Go! Follow your heart and do what you feel is right. If everything goes wrong, you always have me here waiting for you with open arms." Permission. With that sentence, my mother released me from my torture by permitting me to fail.

The gift the universe gave me that day was making me believe I had no other choice but to take this immediate action, to act on this inspired thought that if I vanished from this place, my life would be better.

RISK PLUS ACTION EQUALS GROWTH

When I finally arrived in Bangkok, I couldn't wait to get off the plane and see the blue ocean and white sandy beaches and drink my first coconut water. Except when I stepped off the plane all I could see were high-rise buildings and traffic like I had never experienced. Buildings, cars, storefronts, and thousands of people greeted me as I searched for the paradise I had pictured in my mind. No oceans, no beaches, and no palm trees. I had spent days partying with my friends before leaving home but had done not one minute of research on the country where I would be living. I arrived with only $100 to my name, all that was left of my grandfather's inheritance.

Phuket was so far south that I needed another plane ticket to get there; it cost more than I had.

You get exactly what you ask for, so ask wisely.

I found myself buying a $50 ticket for an eighteen-hour bus ride to Phuket at the advice of the only travel agent who spoke my language. With little choice and nowhere to go, I arrived early to the bus departure hall and sat down on one of the public benches across from the bus station.

Two benches away were two guys drinking some form of liquor. It did not take long until they waved at me to come over and join them. This scenario was familiar to me, drinking in the streets with "friends," so I immediately joined them.

As I told them my story, they reassured me that traveling to Phuket was a good idea because there was much money in that region, and many *farangs* (Thai for "tourists").

Next, they asked me if I had ever tried Thai whiskey before, which they call *lao khao*, meaning fermented rice. They explained that it was delicious and very strong. I was about to board a bus for eighteen hours and start my new life; this seemed like a perfectly good reason to celebrate—plus it would help me sleep better on the bus, I told myself.

One sip soon became two, which then became ten. The next thing I remember is waking up in a moving vehicle, in darkness. Using my cell phone for a light, I looked around to see that bags and suitcases surrounded me.

Again, I was in a total panic. Why was this happening *to* me? My mind raced, and my breathing became irregular. All I could do was look around with the dim light of my cell phone. As I looked around, I realized that I was lying on a white blanket with bags and suitcases packed around me. I finally understood that I was in the luggage compartment below the bus.

It was not until the bus stopped for dinner that the driver opened the hatch and I crawled out, looking very confused and lost. The bus driver explained to me that I had gotten so drunk that I had passed out on the bench where I was drinking with the guys I had just met. When my bus finally arrived at the departure hall, they couldn't wake me up to board the bus. The fermented rice alcohol had left me completely unresponsive.

The bus driver explained that the guys I had been drinking with knew that I was going to Phuket, so they convinced him to take me on that bus. Worried I'd be sick on the bus or disturb other passengers, the driver agreed to let me ride in the luggage compartment. Instead of carrying me onto the bus, they prepared a white blanket on the floor of the luggage compartment with a pillow and placed all the bags and suitcases around me, so I would not roll around.

At the time, I believed that being made to ride to Phuket in the luggage compartment was another thing that was happening *to* me, and I could not see why. I made no connection between my choices and the outcomes. When I reflect on that experience, I realize that it was the most comfortable bus ride I have ever taken in my life, and those two guys who I never saw again saved me by getting the driver to take me on the bus. When the bus driver put me in the luggage compartment it was an act of kindness. The universe was introducing me to the kindness and generosity of the people in Thailand, the country I soon called home.

PUT YOUR LIFE INTO ACTION

Arriving in Phuket with only $40, I was filled with both excitement and panic. I was ready to start my new life in this beautiful place but knew that I needed to find a job quickly.

I approached all the hotels along the beach roads to see if any of them needed a young, motivated worker who spoke three languages fluently. On the second day, I obtained a trial employment opportunity. It was a meager-paying job distributing invitations to tourists to visit a hotel and telling them about the hotel's latest promotions and travel packages. Each time a tourist came in with one of my invitation cards, I would receive a small commission. I now had a job in Thailand. The irony was that I was handing out brochures and talking to people about the beauty and fun to be found in Phuket as if I had lived my entire life there—but I had yet to experience any of this.

With that first job, I rented a tiny room with a fan, a bed, and a shower. I was only making the equivalent of $15-$30 a week, just enough to pay for my tiny room and eat a portion of soup every day, but I was happy. I finally had my blue ocean, white sandy beaches, and coconut trees. I had taken action in my life, and it was finally paying off. All I had to do now was keep going.

RISK AND FAILURE

At the time, I had a budget of 100 Baht a day (about $3). It covered my daily serving of noodle soup (30 Baht) and gas for the rented bike I needed to get to work each day (50 Baht). I used the remaining 20 Baht to refill my phone's SIM card with credit for the day. I was spending money on booze instead of paying my rent. I could only afford one bowl of noodle soup a day. Then I started to ask the friendly Thai lady working the noodle shop if I could eat there and pay later.

Even with such generosity, I awoke one morning with a banging on my door and three police officers on the other side. They had come to evict me.

I owed money to every person I knew, and there was no one to turn to for help. I wouldn't dare call my parents and tell them I had failed again. I was just too proud. So here I was, heavily in debt, and now homeless to boot.

The beauty of Phuket Island is that there are sixteen white sandy beaches. Wherever you live on the island, you're always close to a beach. My first thought was to go down to the nearest beach with my two bags of clothes, sit under a palm tree in the shade, and figure out what to do with this new situation that life had put me in. From my rented room, the nearest beach was not more than five hundred meters away.

The first day and night under the palm tree with my two bags turned into several. Was moving here, ending up like this, worth the risk?

> *Failure both hardens your spirit and teaches you lessons. Success comes when you soften and apply the lessons.*

TAKE ACTION

Most people are afraid of failure, but what they are terrified of is being done, of just rolling over and letting go of their dreams. They're scared of the challenges, of not succeeding as soon as they'd like. What most people don't realize is that the moment they are about to succeed, they pull back. They begin to doubt. They begin to fear, and that's when they genuinely fail. If we look at failure, at setbacks, or challenges as learning opportunities, then we never indeed fail. Even though my initial twenty-plus business ideas didn't turn into complete success, I learned from those experiences to create nineteen very successful business opportunities.

THE SCIENCE OF RISK

There are numerous examples where even a simple assessment of risk would have killed a business idea that turned out to be a huge success.

What to consider when taking a risk:

- Your brain can perceive risk based on emotion or logic.

- Reminding yourself that taking a risk can be a good thing, as it reduces anxiety.

- Learning to bounce back from failure helps improve your confidence when taking future risks.

Research tells us that the decision-making centers of our brain are composed of two kinds of cells: excitatory and inhibitory. Excitatory cells make up roughly 80 percent of this part of the brain, and inhibitory cells make up the remaining 20 percent.[2] When we are younger, we don't have the experiences to put up roadblocks with our excitatory cells, which is why children and teenagers often don't think twice about risky behavior. With age comes experience; this experience becomes a filter that shuts down risky behavior because our brain assigns emotions to our past experiences.

Author Kayt Sukel devotes a section of *The Art of Risk* to the young brain, particularly the mind of the notoriously risky teenager. She details research on sex hormones, the insula brain region, and how teens respond to "good idea/bad idea" questions. Sukel cites fascinating studies that reveal things like how it takes adolescents longer than adults to answer questions such as, "Is it a good or bad idea to eat a cockroach?" Teens typically have to think more because they have less experience and are open to different possibilities, making them less likely to say "bad" immediately.[3] Reading this research made me understand my wild pranks in school and my gang life in Stockholm.

THE ART OF RISK-TAKING

Understand how your brain is perceiving the risk. Recent brain science tells us risk-taking may be conscious or unconscious.[4] When

---

2   György Buzsáki, Kai Kaila, and Marcus Raichle, "Inhibition and Brain Work," *Neuron* 56, no. 5, December 6, 2007: 771-783, doi: 10.1016/j.neuron.2007.11.008.

3   Kayt Sukel, *The Art of Risk: The New Science of Courage, Caution & Chance* (Washington, DC: National Geographic, 2016).

4   Srini Pillay, "A Better Way to Think about Risk," *Harvard Business Review*, December 23, 2014, https://hbr.org/2014/12/a-better-way-to-think-about-risk.

it is unconscious, you may not be aware of the threat or how you are viewing it. Feelings or emotions can obscure critical, rational thinking, or they can promote it. Even if we're conscious of our feelings, we are not aware of how much impact our subconscious emotion has on our desire to take a risk.

Research also shows that people who are sociable, impulsive sensation-seekers or aggressive may be especially likely to take risks.[5] If you compare Mark Zuckerberg, the "college kid lacking business sense" who started Facebook, to the professional managers at NewsCorp, who ran Myspace like a business, it is clear whose risk tolerance paid off. Being a risk taker means you are passionate about what you are doing, so it is generally tied to powerful emotions.

The brain is rigged for error-based learning, which is why we naturally learn from experimentation. Steve Blank, the CEO of Rocket Science Games who was going to revolutionize the video game industry, lost $35 million in funding. Instead of quitting, he went on to start another company, Epiphany, which netted each of its investors $1 billion.

CREATE HAPPINESS AND CONFIDENCE

Taking responsibility can be embarrassing, humbling, painful, and even costly. However, accepting responsibility for your choices can also be very empowering.

Taking personal responsibility means not blaming others for your unhappiness. It means figuring out ways you can be happy despite others' (negative) behaviors and despite external circumstances.

---

5   Marvin Zuckerman, "Are You a Risk Taker?" PsychologyToday, November 1, 2000, https://www.psychologytoday.com/us/articles/200011/are-you-risk-taker.

When I was in a gang, drinking and fighting on the streets of Stockholm, I did not believe I had any control over my life, and I blamed the outcomes of my choices on everyone around me. I was depressed and unhappy because I thought I had no control over my life. One way to take responsibility is to change your emotional response and connection to an event. When I was fired from my jobs, I felt angry and thought I did not deserve it because my boss did not care about me. Had I instead acknowledged that my boss saw I was unhappy at the job, given my actions—and that he was releasing me to find a job that was more fulfilling because he cared about me—then I would feel grateful and more positive about my next steps. Of course, taking responsibility for not showing up to work on time and getting fired, then feeling grateful about being fired, takes effort. It is worthwhile to learn how to control your emotional mind like this.

MENTAL CONTROL LEADS TO CONFIDENCE

Just as a child cannot imagine being as physically strong as an adult, those of us who haven't developed the ability to interpret hardship in a happiness-embracing fashion cannot imagine being happy in extremely negative circumstances.

It is useful to think of the ability to control your emotional response to a specific event as a muscle. Just as your biceps become stronger only when you exercise them, if you allow relatively minor incidents—like an encounter with a rude waitress—to spoil your mood, how can you expect to maintain your happiness when a more extreme event—like a weeklong visit from an unpleasant relative—happens?

A critical element in developing mental control is a willingness to accept whatever comes your way. If you cannot fully accept your results, including, for example, a toxic boss or poor health, then you will not be able to interpret these outcomes in a positive light and, hence, you cannot be happy. So, taking personal responsibility for your happiness involves, ultimately, the willingness to fully and unquestioningly accept the outcomes you are dealt in life.

The more we do this, the more confidence we develop to take new actions to rebound from and move on. More confidence also improves our ability to take risks.

ACT "AS IF"

The Victorian philosopher William James theorized about emotion and behavior. James stated that it isn't our feelings that guide our actions (feel happy and you will laugh). On the contrary, it is our actions that guide our emotions (laugh and you will feel happy). "If you want a quality, act as if you already have it," he concluded.

The same advice applies to almost all aspects of our everyday lives. By acting as if you are a specific type of person, you become that person—what is called the "As If" principle.

—

FOCUS ON "I AM"

*Thoughts become things. If you see it in your
mind, you will hold it in your hand.*

—**Bob Proctor,** *You Were Born Rich*

After being thrown out of my tiny room in Thailand, I spent days sleeping on the beach using my bags as pillows and my two towels as blankets. I made sure to wake up at five o'clock, just before the first tourists or workers arrived, so they did not see me. I spent nights looking at the stars trying to understand how I had ended up under these palm trees. Some nights I cried myself to sleep, and other nights I raged and blamed my company, my parents, and my friends for my situation. I blamed everyone and everything for ending up homeless—except myself.

One afternoon while sitting on the beach, I was hungry and desperately trying to figure out how I could get food. I had borrowed money from everyone I knew in the area and the only person willing to extend me credit was the lovely lady at the noodle shop. Over the years she would become a second mother to me as I would recount my life to her over a bowl of hot noodles. However, even with her kindness, I was tired of noodles and was starving in many ways. Then an idea flashed in my mind, reminding me of an old friend in Sweden whom I had not talked to since I'd left. I called him. I started to beg him to help me so I could afford to get a cheap room somewhere. He listened to me, and when I finished my story, he told me that he could not help me with money but would email me a book that he thought could help me. Wow!

Here I was homeless with nothing, and he was offering me a book! A book that was going to help me? I was asking for money because that is what I needed to get food and a room. A book! I couldn't believe it. I was also embarrassed, and so I thanked him for offering to send me the book.

I hung up, angry and upset that his only offer of help was to send me a book. I realized after a few hours that a book would help me pass the time in the evenings with nothing else to do sitting on the beach. Maybe this book would focus my mind on something other than dwelling on how life was being cruel to me. I printed it out at the local internet shop and started reading it that very same night.

For those of you who've read *The Secret: The Law of Attraction* or at least heard about it, you'd expect that I would have had an epiphany right there on the beach, that the book would have been the key to turning my life around, but it wasn't. My first reactions to reading the book: Unrealistic. Garbage. I was so angry at my friend that I decided to take this anger out on the book.

Think positive.

Visualize, and you will receive.

What a load of crap!

I set out to prove the theories in *The Secret* were wrong. I would follow the book's instructions to the letter, and I would prove they did not work.

I started to visualize small because I didn't believe it would work and it seemed easier to follow the instructions using small things. A cup of coffee. I sat on my towel on the beach and decided to focus my mind with closed eyes, thinking deeply how great it would feel to have someone give me a cup of hot, delicious coffee. The first few times I tried it I felt stupid, but with little else to do on that beach I kept trying. After a few more attempts I began to see the cup of coffee more clearly in my head. I could see the steam rising from the cup; I could smell the aroma. Two days later while sitting on the beach, one of the beach boys who handled the jet skis came up to me and said, "I've seen you several days here already, so I thought I could offer you a coffee. You look very tired."

I couldn't believe it! Not only had I manifested what I saw in my mind, but it was the best cup of coffee I'd had in a long time.

Still skeptical but more curious, I decided I would manifest lunch. I had not eaten anything but noodles in weeks, and the thought of a good lunch seemed like a massive windfall to me. When I closed my eyes and began the visualization exercise, I still felt silly. The first few times were awkward and stiff. With the memory of the coffee, I kept trying until I could feel myself eating the lunch.

A few days later, I bumped into an old colleague from the hotel.

"Hi, Andres," he said. "I have not seen you for a while. How are you? Let me buy you lunch!"

Was this working or was this a coincidence? Regardless of the first two visualizations coming to fruition, I was still not entirely convinced and decided I would increase the stakes. I would visualize something bigger and more complex—like getting a better job! I started visualizing how good it would feel to have a job where I could get paid and be able to afford a room to sleep in again and have daily showers, clean new clothes, and a better life—a life that would make my parents proud.

VISUALIZING WITH EMOTION

I was visualizing vivid pictures and creating movies in my mind about the new job I wanted in my life, but it was not until much later that I understood that any creative visualization needs to be backed by strong positive emotions. That's where the real magnetism and attraction happen. I was lucky that I was doing it unintentionally in the beginning.

Of course, I didn't just sit and wait on the beach feeling happy about getting a new job; I had to take action. I spent two days asking around town about job openings. On the second day, I landed a job as a marketing executive, handing tourists brochures from a real estate office. After a few short weeks, instead of a tiny room to rent, I could afford a nice little house with a small garden in the back.

I now wanted to read many other books, and I filled my spare time reading book after book on the power of the mind. Using the cup of coffee, the lunch, and the new job as my proof that I could finally have control over my own life, I started to implement into my life many of the teachings from the books I was reading. Did I finally have control over my life because I was beginning to think differently, or had I previously been giving up control over my life by not thinking differently?

The answer is less important than the act of merely starting to think differently. With my newfound excitement for life, I began using daily affirmations after learning the power of auto-suggestions by Napoleon Hill in his book, *Think and Grow Rich*. I learned to program my subconscious mind into whatever I wished to achieve, experience, or have during meditation sessions, which I read about from others like Tony Robbins and Jack Canfield. I also began writing down my goals daily and placing the pieces of paper all over my apartment and office.

Things started to happen in my life very quickly as I became better and better at creative visualizations, calming my mind, and writing down daily goals. My life changed because of my daily morning routine of sitting in my garden, visualizing all my goals and events that I wanted to materialize. On the way to work, I would repeat my affirmations loudly. I would sit in my car and yell, "I'm the best salesperson in Thailand! Everyone who meets me loves to buy from me! I create my reality! I am a master salesman! I am a successful person! I am a happy and helping person! I am in the process of becoming wealthy!" I finally felt in control of my life, and it motivated me to keep pushing harder and taking more and more action.

The feelings you dream up in your mind around people, places, and things are the most powerful ingredients for creating your best reality.

THE POWER OF "I AM"

One of the things that I have added to the knowledge I learned over sixteen years from all these books and seminars is the power of *I am.* Adding the words "I am" in front of any affirmation enhances it since you talk directly with your soul, which connects directly with your subconscious and conscious thoughts. It is through this process of auto-suggestions that I was able to remaster my life.

On my living room and bedroom walls I have the same script that I repeat every day, and during the day my subconscious sees it on the wall and takes notice of it.

The painted inscriptions are:

I AM whole.

I AM healthy.

I AM happy.

I AM wealthy.

I AM helpful.

Sometimes I repeat these five focus points more than a hundred times on days when I am working on a big project in my business. While this may seem silly or a waste of time to you, consider that if you can control your mind, you can control your life. Your mind is mostly a subconscious machine when you consider all of the things it has you do without conscious thought, like breathing. Focusing forces the mind to reprogram itself.

Your conscious mind is very protective as to what it will let into your supercomputer, the subconscious mind. It acts like a twenty-four-hour security guard, making sure nothing enters without proper reason.

Daily affirmations are very important to keep your mood elevated and your subconscious programmed with the right thinking and behaviors you need to achieve your deepest desires. Adding *I am* to my daily affirmations made all the difference.

FIVE MAIN "I AM" POINTS OF FOCUS

There are endless possibilities to what you can center your affirmations around. I have found that by limiting it to these specific five, I can intensify my focus and get faster, more meaningful results.

I AM whole: I have chosen "I AM whole" since I'm deeply grateful that I'm a whole person with no handicaps, and I wish to continue being whole. Some people have physical disadvantages. Some people battle with depression, anxiety, or confidence issues. I remember battling depression, paranoia, and anxiety; I was not whole then. In this respect, I am now a whole person and choose to be conscious and grateful for this. I also acknowledge that because I am whole I have little right to complain or make excuses and I have to help others in need.

I AM healthy: This is another statement that has a powerful meaning, since nothing in this world can be of much pleasure if you have a sick body. Exercising and following a nutritious diet are essential to being healthy, so this is a prime focus in my life. I've found that when I focus on my health, it is then easier to concentrate on my other goals of success.

I AM happy: "I AM happy" is a fundamental key to my success and achievement. We should always be programming our mind to have a happy and positive outlook so we can enjoy what we do and have in life. Focusing on being happy makes us more productive, grateful, and open to new experiences.

I AM wealthy: "I AM wealthy," as I have stated previously, comes from the fact that we need to create what we want in our minds first before it can manifest in our physical world. Your mind needs to accept the concept of wealth, free from limiting beliefs and self-doubt. We can only become that through constant repetition until our subconscious mind has taken it as being true with no restrictions. Our world has abundant wealth, and anyone can share in that abundance with the right state of mind to receive it.

I AM helpful: This has always been a significant statement for me. There is no greater feeling than helping others in need without expecting anything in return. You don't need to know a person to help them, and there are always people in need everywhere—you need to put in a little effort to find them.

I have chosen these five affirmations because they represent what is most important to me, and they are the characteristics I desire to continue having throughout my whole life. What will be your five?

I have kept myself motivated by using this method and by continuously programming my mind, my soul, and my belief system by repeating these statements and forming this practice into habit and routine. Of course, I've had my ups and downs and sometimes weeks can pass by without me practicing my affirmations, but I gently guide myself back to the practice.

MEDITATION AND VISUALIZATION

Often when my employees have downturns or less productive months, I ask them if they have set any new goals for themselves or if they have glanced at or read their goals that month. I also ask them if they are reading any books and, if so, which ones? Then I like to ask when they last did affirmations. Usually asking these questions gets them to realize that they have fallen out of a routine, and it's enough to kick-start their successful habits again.

One way that I make sure to repeat my daily affirmations is by creating a physical reminder of my visualizations during meditation. When I first started in real estate sales and was trying to achieve deals, I would start by writing one letter or two on my hands. For instance, every time I was in the car headed for the real estate office, I would look down at my hands on the steering wheel and see "bs," which stood for "best salesperson." I would then repeat to myself, "I'm the best salesperson in Phuket." Or when I wanted to have a new car, a Toyota Vios, I wrote "tv" on my hand so that every time I saw those letters, I would repeat to myself, "I'm driving a Toyota Vios." If someone asked about the writing on my hand, I would say that it was an appointment I need to remember. So, no matter where you are going for the day, make sure to have small cues to help remind yourself of your affirmations and to program yourself with those positive thoughts.

PRINCIPLE #4

—

THINKING TIME: MAKE IT A PRIORITY

Be alone, that is the secret of invention; be alone, that is when ideas are born.

—Nikola Tesla

The first business I ever owned was the real estate agency I launched after resigning as sales director from the real estate office where I had started. During those first few years, I'd saved enough to open my own little real estate office. I was now an independent business owner. My confidence was high. But while in my mind I was on my way to incredible success in real estate, I still had a lot to learn about running a business.

Several months into managing the agency, I started to struggle again. I had very few clients and sales revenue was down. I needed to pay my office rental fees, suppliers for marketing material, and two employees. I started to borrow money to pay bills. That was the beginning of another downward spiral.

MY WORST BUSINESS "FAILURE"

I wasn't making enough money. My debts were starting to mount. I was two months late with the office rent. I could not pay my two employees. To make matters worse, I received a phone call from the building owners telling me I had to pack and leave, as they were going to rent the space to another business.

I had to declare to the bank that I was bankrupt.

I had to face my employees and tell them we were going out of business and that I wouldn't be able to pay their salary. These employees trusted me. Relied on me. Supported me and had families who relied on them. This was one of the hardest moments I ever faced in my life.

My agency officially closed. I started to ask myself, "Why did this happen? Where did it go wrong? How could it happen? What situations led to this, and what can I do to make it better?"

LEARNING FROM MISTAKES

My first mistake was acquiring office space in a remote part of town where no clients or buyers would visit. I leased this particular office space because it was big and cheap. My thinking was to go big at first, so I could occupy the office with more employees and more computers and make it impressive for clients when they did visit us. I soon discovered (one of my failures) that I should have focused on lining up clients and customers before I started expanding. Marketing should always come first, impressive office space later. With no clients, you have no sales. Without sales, you have no income. With no income, you don't have anything when it comes to business.

I wrote down all the things that went wrong and how they went wrong. My first realization: I had stopped creating goals for myself. Without consciously doing so, I had quit my daily habits of affirmations, visualizations, and meditation when I opened my first company. I had stopped reading self-development books and listening to audio tapes and other motivational products and materials. I became caught in the mental prison of worrying about all the things that I didn't want in my life again. I focused on sadness and scarcity instead of happiness and abundance.

That evening I took my pen out and started to write down all my goals and desires, from minor to major. When I finished, I realized that I had not visualized for almost a year. Could it have that big of an impact in my life?

I migrated to my backyard garden. There sat my old chair right where I left it over a year ago, deteriorated from the sun and rain. It struck me that, just like the old chair, I had become worn and tired from neglecting to do all the things that had brought me so much happiness. I started to meditate again, and after just one session I was filled with calm and was much clearer on what I wanted to be, do, or have in my life. I wrote down affirmations and applied my auto-suggestions backed by positive feelings. My walls were once again beginning to become covered in A4 sheets with strong affirmations written all over them. Pictures of materialistic things started to go up in my house and fridge again, so I could start seeing the things I wanted daily. I was operating from an abundance mindset again.

I had no office and no employees, but I still had my marketing booth in a six-meter square space at our local shopping mall. I started my mornings in my garden thinking of how great it would be with happy clients who loved buying real estate from me. My deep morning meditations filled me with a newly awakened passion. Two months before the next payment on my house was due, I started to get sales and earn income again.

It did not take long until I had a solid database of buyers and investors who urged me to develop a condominium project. I had gained their trust and respect after placing their funds in high-yielding property investments. It was natural to say yes because I had long been visualizing the goal of becoming a property developer!

Crisis enters our life because we lose personal focus and inner confidence. When handling an emergency, we often look for outside verification that everything will be all right. We go outward instead of inward, which creates additional stress and anxiety. A crisis causes us to lose touch with what we want and confidence in our ability to obtain it.

THINKING TIME

I love nature. I love climbing mountains, and I love spending days in the wild, far away from civilization, unable to check my emails or even make a phone call. Acknowledging that the world can survive without you for several days is the first step in being able to detach and focus inward. That's how I reload myself with new energy and motivation and I learn to love life itself. I believe connecting with nature is essential to our spirits. We disconnect from the energy of the earth itself in today's modern world, which has made us lose part of our spirituality. We came from nature, we are a part of it, and when you spend days out in nature, you will feel comfort and bliss. Nature itself is talking to you when you pay attention and stay in the present moment. It is where I go for my thinking time.

Taking time to be alone doesn't mean you must be lonely. It merely says you are focusing on yourself, the one who should mean the most to you in this world. It's important to have people in your life whom you love, but you should never put others before yourself to the point where you are then living a miserable experience. Instead, take time out of every day just for you. You can spend the time meditating, going for a walk, doing a bit of retail therapy, or working on your dream board or goal list. Whatever you choose to do during the time you give yourself each day, make sure that the activity will benefit you in some way, whether that is to still your mind, relax your body, or help you focus on what you want to accomplish next. It should be a time when fear and worry cannot affect you, and it should leave you feeling recharged and ready to go back to whatever you need to do next to achieve your dreams.

RESPONSE TIME

One of the main things I learned in business is that when a crisis hits, our instinct is to fight or flee, just like in nature. If a business deal is going badly, we immediately ask ourselves, "Should I fight to win, or should I walk away?" When you are facing a downturn in sales, a bad apple employee, competitors stealing your business, tax issues, or funding problems, it is comfortable to stop thinking of solutions and start focusing on fight or flight responses. When you are in fight or flight mode, having thinking time and being alone is very challenging. Since I spent many years in this reactionary mode, I became a student of how to avoid this state of being—and relax.

The founder of Harvard's Institute for Mind Body Medicine, Dr. Herbert Benson, coined the term "Relaxation Response." The response defines your personal ability to encourage your body to release chemicals and brain signals that slow down your muscles and organs and increase blood flow to the brain. It is essentially the opposite reaction to the "fight or flight" response. The Relaxation Response is essentially a form of deep relaxation, which affects and activates the parasympathetic nervous system, and you practice it through activities such as visualization, meditation, affirmations, breathing techniques, and yoga.

His studies throughout the 1960s and 1970s indicated that normal secretion of stress hormones contributes to many medical conditions such as cardiovascular disease, GI diseases, and adrenal fatigue. His research has also shown that regular use of the Relaxation Response can help relieve stress-related health problems, including insomnia and hypertension.[6]

BEING ALONE IS A FORM OF SELF-CARE

Finding time to be with yourself helps you practice self-care, an excellent technique for focusing on yourself and what you want to achieve in this lifetime. When you can love yourself fully, then you can genuinely love another person. Spending time alone doesn't mean you're selfish. It merely says you're dedicated, both to yourself and to those you serve. You are becoming the best version of yourself when you dedicate the time as often as you can to do things that bring you peace and love. You are your own biggest fan and the most

---

6   Marilyn Mitchell, "Dr. Herbert Benson's Relaxation Response," Psychology Today, March 29, 2013, https://www.psychologytoday.com/us/blog/heart-and-soul-healing/201303/dr-herbert-benson-s-relaxation-response.

motivating person in your life. It's important to take care of number one—you—and allow yourself to feel whole again.

The biggest breakthroughs come from solitude.

PRINCIPLE #5

—

CELEBRATION CREATES ADDICTION TO PROGRESS

Colleagues should take care of each other, have fun, celebrate success, learn by failure, look for reasons to praise others and not to criticize. Communicate freely and respect each other.

—**Richard Branson**

Before I arrived in Thailand, I remember mostly darkness. I tried to leave the streets of my gang family to work at a job that was supposed to put me on the right path. I left the comfort of the streets I knew, the camaraderie, the feeling of being a part of something—even if it was the wrong thing. On the streets, when I would win a fight, my street family would be excited for me. I felt the impact I had on the streets, and it came back to me in positive vibrations, which is one reason I was loyal to my gang life for so long, even though it almost killed me.

In Stockholm, sitting at my desk at the telemarketing firm, surrounded by other people all day, I felt utterly alone and worthless. When I would close a sale, there was always someone else getting praised for closing a more significant sale. The bonuses went to the top closers, and the rest of us went unrecognized. In this company, the best got praised and the worst were asked to leave, while those of us in the middle were invisible.

I've said before that I hated that telemarketing job so much that, after being late so often, I was let go, leaving me paranoid staring through the peephole of my apartment. Was this job responsible for my anxiety, depression, and lack of motivation? No, ultimately that was on me. However, was the job responsible for making me feel invisible, unimportant, and replaceable?

With nineteen companies and hundreds of employees in all different types of businesses from real estate to gyms to coffee shops, I have experienced great success. A large part of that success is building teams that always feel seen, heard, and irreplaceable.

In that telemarketing office, the awards went to individuals: the employee of the month or the person with the top sales figures. This rewards system always struck me as demotivating. Management only valued the employees who were continually winning. There were no team achievements nor acknowledgment for the employees who supported the top salespeople. I watched good people quit, and many, like me, became isolated and performed at lower levels. The only thing I learned from that job was that teams matter. People deserve to be recognized.

For every victory, let there be a celebration. Taking the time to recognize your successes will immediately boost positivity and vanquish negativity. You may not want to throw a party for every single accomplishment, but at least acknowledge it to yourself, pat yourself on the back, and smile about it.

In my teen years and in my early years in Phuket, I took the celebration to a whole new level. As a youth, every night was a party to celebrate life, because who knew what was going to happen tomorrow. All my money went to buying alcohol and spending time with my friends. Even when I first moved to Thailand and got my first job at the hotel, just passing out promotional material, I took what very little money I was earning and started to party again with coworkers who had the same perspective on life. Celebrating with your friends or even coworkers once in a while in this way is fine, but you shouldn't make it a daily habit or the primary focus in your life.

Small mistakes almost always make us feel bad. So, accomplishing small goals should always make us feel good!

CELEBRATE SUCCESSES WITH OTHERS

Show enthusiasm—always. All of this is more important and more fun than you think. Don't take yourself so seriously. Loosen up, and everybody around you will loosen up. Have fun.

Create great teamwork by organizing outings for your employees. Whenever my sales team breaks a record or hits targets, we celebrate. We plan an outing together as a team and enjoy our moments of victory and teamwork. Great feelings of accomplishment overcome the team members, and they realize that it's much more fun and productive to celebrate success with others than to be alone. I implore employees to celebrate, and to be happy when they hear of others' accomplishments ... even if they see them as rivals.

In 2016, my sales team and I broke a long-lasting sales record we had been trying to break for almost two years, and upon that accomplishment, I invited the whole sales team to climb to the top of one of Southeast Asia's highest active volcanos! Our spirits filled with joy, relief, and happiness. We bonded after that four-day extreme summit. We shared tents, sat around campfires, and shared stories about ourselves. Our teams have become so caring and helpful toward each other that they are surpassing previous records and revenues.

CELEBRATE EVERYDAY THINGS

Take the time to celebrate the small things every day; this goes hand in hand with finding little things to be grateful for. Celebrate a home-cooked meal you made, a successful day at work, or perhaps a new business relationship that you didn't have before. Celebrations shouldn't be limited to when your business has made an enormous breakthrough or sale. Celebrate the small things too, like employees' birthdays or wedding anniversaries. Know your employees. Don't just celebrate the organization's success, but also individual success in everyone's lives.

You can celebrate in small ways or in big ways. You can merely meditate and reflect on what you were able to accomplish, or go out to a concert and celebrate life with everyone dancing around you. Take the time to celebrate with other people and maximize the feeling of joy and accomplishment. The key is that, when you include others in your celebration, you should be conscious of their emotional experience and plan something that everyone will enjoy.

CREATE ADDICTION TO PROGRESS

Teresa Amabile, a Harvard Business School professor, led a study that analyzed twelve thousand diary entries from 238 employees at seven companies.[7] The findings were fascinating.

Workers' motivation was enhanced when they wrote down their achievements daily in the diary. The practice of recording our progress, Amabile explains, helps us appreciate small wins, which in turn boosts our confidence.

Confidence is the key to achieving future, more considerable successes.

This research and an article by Patrik Edblad showed me that, no matter how small, acknowledging accomplishments triggers the reward center of our brains. Our brain releases what I call "happy hormones," which are essential chemicals that when released give us a feeling of achievement and pride.[8]

One of those hormones, the neurotransmitter dopamine, is the chemical that gives us that sweet feeling of reward but also pushes us to act on what triggered its release in the first place.

I was surprised to discover that the same substance that gets people hooked on gambling, nicotine, and alcohol essentially creates an addiction to progress. Being from the streets, this "addiction to progress" concept made perfect sense to me.

---

7   Teresa Amabile and Steven J. Kramer, "The Power of Small Wins," *Harvard Business Review*, May 2011.

8   Patrik Edblad, "How to Stay Motivated: The Art and Science of Leveraging Small Wins," *Productive! Magazine* no. 21, accessed February 2019, http://productivemag.com/21/how-to-stay-motivated-the-art-science-of-leveraging-small-wins.

PRINCIPLE #6

—

THE LAW OF VIBRATIONAL GIVING

*If you knew what I know about the power
of giving, you would not let a single meal
pass without sharing it in some way.*

—Siddhartha Gautama

Most people know that giving can lead to receiving. Success masters like John Grey, Jack Canfield, and Tony Robbins teach about the Law of Attraction as it pertains to giving: that what you give you will get back tenfold in return. While I am a big believer in the principle that the universe returns to you tenfold what you send out into it, in my opinion, most people are going about giving in the wrong way. The act of giving is as simple as giving away money to someone who needs it with a sense of spiritual duty or responsibility. I believe the act of giving should be in the form of "vibrational giving." What's the difference?

Traditional giving: The way most people give is by tithing. That is the conventional way of giving ten percent of your income to a religious organization. Most religions teach that we need to give ten percent of the money we receive as a form of "payment" to God. While that has worked for centuries, and I have no argument with it, it's just not the way I do it.

Dr. Joe Vitale tells people to give ten percent of their income to wherever they receive spiritual nourishment. That could be an Uber driver, a waiter, someone you meet at the store who says encouraging words, or an organization. I like this idea because it opens the possibility of giving to others, including, but not limited to, a church.

Responsibility or duty-based giving: When we donate money (and perhaps time) to charities, action groups, or impact organizations like Toys for Tots, the Girl Scouts, or the Red Cross, we are doing so out of a sense of responsibility or duty. We feel obligated to support a cause we identify with in some way. Again, this is not how I believe we should practice giving.

Vibrational giving: I discovered a specific way of giving that resulted in me becoming a billionaire before the age of thirty-five. I focus on the emotion that I feel while I am doing the giving. The feeling attached to the giving is far more critical than most people may realize. If you feel hate as you do anything, you are setting up an "attractor field" to experience hate later. If you feel love as you do something, you are also engaging in a principle to attract love back to you later. The trouble is, most people give only money and expect only money in return. While that works, it's limited. The universe may have something better for you than money. I've learned that this "vibrational giving" is the real secret to giving.

Give, and the universe will give back to you tenfold.

GIVE, WITHOUT EXPECTATION

I once did a fourteen-day trek across India with my friend David (in a rickshaw, I might add) to raise money for Cool Earth, a charity that buys rainforest areas in South America to preserve and make sure they never get cut down. We drove through the whole of northern India through some of the poorest cities and towns where many of the locals had never even seen a tourist. We were a strange sight to say the least: a bald, white, English man (David) and a Latino-looking guy (me) riding through town on a homemade motorized rickshaw that continually broke down, leaving us perplexed about how to fix it. However, every time, within moments, a group of townspeople would come over, inspect the vehicle, and manage to fix the problem. Every time after getting help, we reached for our wallets to give them a tip for their much-appreciated work, and each time they declined. They did it out of pure human heart and kindness. Indians, as well, are one of the most friendly and helpful people I have ever met. They reinforced the law of vibrational giving.

GIVE THAT EMOTION, RECEIVE THAT EMOTION

When I wish someone a good day, I do it with genuine feelings of wanting that person to have a good day. Most people say, "Have a good day," with no feeling at all. It's automatic. It's dead. The feeling I put behind "good day" is love as I say the words to the other person. This is intentional. As a result, what I expect to get back is the feeling of love. It may come as great news about a project, or a check, or a profitable idea, or a new connection, or some other reason to celebrate, but I give out love and what I get back is love.

When you give money and feel ecstatic, what you will receive in return is something with the feeling of ecstasy attached to it. This may come back to you in the form of money, but it could be anything else. You gave with a certain emotion, so what you receive will be the same emotion, but multiplied at least ten times.

Let me share my story of making my first million dollars with this method.

In Thailand, on your birthday you don't receive gifts, you give them. Giving gifts on a birthday rather than receiving gifts was an entirely new concept to me when I first moved to Thailand, but I started practicing it.

Many years ago, on my birthday, I visited an orphanage in Thailand where many of the children had HIV. The orphanage had no government support and was struggling to operate. I wanted to help more than just with the bags of toys I had brought as gifts. I agreed to paint the building and all the rooms at my own cost. I received no money. I did it because I felt great knowing I was helping them.

While I had been visualizing making my first million dollars, I also didn't know how it would happen. When I was at that orphanage, I didn't think spending money there would bring me a million dollars later. All I knew is that these kids needed help and it would make me feel good to help.

I invested about $80,000 in hiring people to paint and rebuild the orphanage. While that was about a fourth of my monthly revenue at the time, spending it didn't make me feel stretched or worried. It made me feel good. My action wasn't calculated; I didn't give money to get money.

Instead, I did something that made me feel great, and I expected something to happen later that would also cause a great feeling, but money wasn't the focus. I just made sure to acknowledge the emotion.

As a result, a few weeks later a deal I had in the works went through. I closed a property worth so much that my commission on it was more than $1 million. Actually, it was $1 million plus about $80,000, so I not only made my first million, but I also recouped my investment in the universe.

The feeling I had when I invested in helping the orphanage (feeling great) came back to me multiplied (feeling fantastic). I copied that check, framed it, and still look at it every day. Is this a coincidence? If it had only happened to me once, then I would think that. I have seen many great things come into my life as a result of vibrational giving. Practicing vibrational giving works for me and will work for you, too. Mother Teresa had it right when she said, "It is not how much we do, but how much love we put in the doing. It is not how much we give, but how much love we put in the giving."

GIVE FIRST OF WHATEVER YOU WISH TO RECEIVE

I started to be successful and wealthy when I applied the mindset of vibrational giving. Anytime I see a beggar on the street I make sure to pull out the largest bill in my wallet. The smile, the surprise, and the emotional reaction that this prompts gives me a great feeling of joy and gratitude. I like to be the one who gives more than expected and with no expectations on how the recipient will use it. If I am giving money to people in need because I want them to use it in a certain way, then I would not be practicing vibrational giving. If I am giving them money because I know the joy and happiness they will feel, then I am practicing vibrational giving.

It is why the Law of Attraction works for some people and not for others. It's about recognizing the emotion behind your actions.

If it's money you seek, make sure to help others make money first. If it's more happiness you want, help others find things to be happy about. If it's a relationship you seek, make sure to be a good friend, listener, and companion as well. It never fails. You have to learn how to read the signals, signs, and hunches when those moments of receiving come back to you. The law of vibrational giving is the core of wealth attraction and creating unlimited opportunity in your life.

BUDDHISM AND GIVING WITH INTENTION

The importance of giving with positive emotion is one of the central practices of Buddhism. Buddha teaches that what is far more important than the gift given is the intention and state of mind in which you give the gift. The karmic benefits amplify after one gives purely. A pure gift is one provided for the proper time, person, and circumstance, and is one earned by honest means. Giving with pure intentions is to provide with compassion—attentively, and without negatively affecting others.

GIVING IS HEALTHY

Being part of something bigger than ourselves might be one of the best things we can do, both for others and ourselves. Studies have shown that having a purpose outside yourself is beneficial for your mental and physical health, longevity, and even your genes.

For example, UCLA researchers looked at both eudaimonic happiness and hedonic happiness.[9] Eudaimonia is a Greek word commonly translated as "happiness" or "welfare"; however, "human flourishing or prosperity" has been proposed as a more accurate translation.

Eudaimonic happiness focuses on meaning and self-realization and defines well-being regarding the degree to which a person is fully functioning.

On the other hand, hedonic happiness is defined by self-gratification, pleasure attainment, and pain avoidance—the kind of happiness you might feel when splurging on something you've had your eye on for a while.

The UCLA researchers linked these two types of happiness with genetic changes and found that eudaimonic happiness was related to lower levels of inflammatory gene expression and higher levels of antibody and antiviral genes. Hedonic happiness had the reverse effect.

GIVING IS ADDICTIVE

The euphoric feeling we experience is known as the "helper's high," a phrase introduced by Allan Luks, a volunteerism and wellness expert. Many researchers have observed the idea of altruism behaving like a miracle drug. Harvard cardiologist Herbert Benson says that "helping others is a door through which one can go to forget oneself and experience our natural hardwired physical sensation."[10]

We've all heard about the "runner's high," the result of endorphin levels rising. Helper's high occurs when people perform good deeds for other people. In other words, it's a classic example of nature's

9   Mark Wheeler, "Be Happy: Your Genes May Thank You for It," UCLA Newsroom, July 29, 2013.

10   Jenny Santi, *The Giving Way to Happiness: Stories and Science Behind the Life-Changing Power of Giving* (New York: Penguin Press, 2016), 9.

built-in reward system for those who help others. After spending so many years finding my "high" in unhealthy ways, I was fascinated by this concept.

A 2007 University of Oregon study explored differences in brain activity when donations were voluntary versus mandatory.[11] Participants were each given $100 and told that nobody would know how much of it they kept or gave away. Not even the researchers who enlisted them and scanned their brains would know. The donation choices were stored on a portable memory drive, and the donations indicated by subjects were then paid in cash or mailed to a charity without knowing who had given what.

An MRI measured the brain responses. Sometimes the subjects were asked to donate some of their cash to a local food bank. Sometimes a tax was levied that sent their money to the food bank without their approval. Sometimes they received extra money, and sometimes the food bank received money without any of it coming from the subjects.

Subjects who voluntarily gave to the food bank experienced a "warm glow." The areas of the brain that release the pleasure chemical dopamine unexpectedly lit up (the caudate, nucleus accumbens, and insula). These are the same areas that respond when you eat a dessert or receive money. I am fascinated by the fact that we are physically hardwired to want to give.

---

11   William T. Harbaugh et al., "Neural Responses to Taxation and Voluntary Giving Reveal Motives for Charitable Donations," *Science* 316, no. 5831 (June 2007): 1622-1625.

GIVING STARTS WITH YOURSELF

Love yourself first so you can give love to others. Alternatively, if it's money you want, help other people make money, and that's what will start to come back to you. The more you do it, the more you'll receive. That is why the law of vibrational giving is one of the essential principles and could be as vital as meditation. Whatever you give, whether small or big, take inspired action and give what feels right. Don't ever give because you expect the universe to pay you back. You must give with good feelings in your heart. Let love be the emotion that governs your thoughts and actions, since love is the most reliable, most powerful emotion in the world. Learning to love yourself first is like finding the meaning of life. Love itself can be a life's purpose, and one that will bring about days filled with joy and happiness.

I know now that the more you give, the more you get, but what about the more you spend? The way I've come to understand the principle of spending money relates to energy. Since everything is a form of energy, that energy can be manipulated, meaning it can be affected. Moreover, the way we change the energy of money is based on the feelings we have when we spend. When we give money, we know that we will receive something in return tenfold. The same principle applies to spending money as well, as long as we infuse the energy of that money with positive vibrations, a positive attitude, and good intentions. When you spend money with that frame of mind, then it will come back to you tenfold.

If you're spending money and worrying, "Oh, maybe this is too much," or, "Maybe I shouldn't have done that," or, "Is this the right thing to do?" or, more importantly, "Will I recover that money again?" then this is an entirely different process. You are sending out the wrong vibrations. You experience worry and fear instead of happiness, peace, and even gratitude. When you spend money with worry in your mind, then you're going to lose the opportunity to receive, to be blessed. When you donate or give with the wrong intention or purpose, you'll receive nothing useful in return.

Therefore, when you give or spend, focus on the right intention and let the universe worry about what you'll receive in return.

GIVING GROWS COMPANIES

Research and consulting firm Great Place to Work conducted a study of several hundred companies and more than 380,000 employees to create its 2018 "Best Workplaces for Giving Back" list. The research found companies that give back to the community have higher employee retention, brand ambassadorship, and employee enthusiasm.[12] Moreover, employees at organizations that give back are thirteen times more likely to look forward to coming to work.[13] Again, even if I did not sincerely believe in the law of vibrational giving and had not reaped the rewards it brought, I would still instill a culture of giving in my companies, as it is proven to increase performance. Giving is, therefore, good business.

Always find a reason to give to others, to strengthen others. In return, you'll succeed in everything you're trying to achieve. Be fair in all your doings and dealings, and the universe will enable your success and happiness.

---

12   Ed Frauenheim, "Why Companies That Give Back Also Receive," *Fortune,* February 9, 2018.

13   Ibid.

PRINCIPLE #7

—

GRATITUDE

A true hero isn't measured by the size of his strength, but by the size of his heart.

—Zeus, Disney's *Hercules*

Learning about visualization taught me the practice of gratitude. Gratitude is a powerful concept advocated by many of the most successful people in the world. If gratitude is essential to them, I decided I should understand why and how to apply it as they do.

The key to the gratitude I found was to let go and stop worrying about the things I did not have in my life; switching my focus to what I *did* have made all the difference. I had to acknowledge that I was thankful for these things. Learning to be thankful every day opened up so many doors of opportunity.

By studying how to apply gratitude in my life, I was able to upgrade my life completely. While I was homeless and handing out brochures for the real estate company, I started to practice gratitude. I would thank the universe for all the things that I had, and I stopped worrying about the things that I didn't have. My life started to get better by the day. I went from being a marketing person giving out brochures in the sun to being a sales executive, then a sales manager, and then a sales director—all in the same company. All of this happened within two years thanks to what I was learning and how I was implementing what I was learning into my life.

Shifting my focus to what I *had* instead of what I didn't have was as simple as flipping on a light switch in my head. I could see how focusing on what I lacked caused me to miss out on the value of what I did have in life.

Instead of dwelling on my lack of money for a plane ticket from Bangkok to Phuket, I was thankful for the bus driver who gave my unconscious, drunk self a chance and a ride on the bus to Phuket.

Instead of focusing on not having enough money to eat, I gave thanks for the noodle soup lady who would make sure that I had something to eat every day, even when I could not pay. The more I thought about the noodle soup lady, I became even more grateful because I realized what an impact she'd had on me.

That noodle soup lady became a significant figure in my early life in Thailand because of the angel that she was. The shop only had four tables with twelve chairs, and most of the time the shop was empty when I went there. When I first started visiting the noodle soup shop and she would give me a free bowl of noodles, I thought she just felt sorry for me because I was needy. There was no doubt that she could see that. Sometimes weeks would go by without me paying her, and she would still serve me my daily bowl of noodle soup. She became a second mom to me, feeding me for almost a year without any guarantee that I could ever pay her back.

What I realized quickly was that she just enjoyed giving to others without asking for anything back. I used to see her smile, which always came with the soup, as a smile of pity. When I focused on the fact that she was giving me a bowl of noodle soup with a smile, rather than on the fact that I couldn't pay her for it, her smile made me feel loved, not pitied. The noodle shop lady was the first person to make me understand the importance of giving without expecting anything in return, and how great embracing gratitude was to being happy and prosperous. She had a heart of gold! I will never forget her for as long as I live.

The sad part is that we eventually lost touch. The shop that I would visit in those early days in Phuket has been empty for years now. I have not seen her in years. However, one of the 101 goals I write each year always includes locating this woman and building her a proper restaurant for her noodle soup. It would mean so much to me to be able to thank her in this way. I visualize that day and seeing her smile again. Whenever I need a reminder of the power of gratitude, I remember her first. Remembering to focus on what you have rather than what you don't is the key to gratitude. You'll be surprised how much you have to be grateful for once you make this mental switch.

Another person I am eternally grateful for is my Swedish friend who first sent me *The Secret*. Rather than focusing on the fact that he would not give me the money I needed, I focused on all the blessings his single act brought me. If it wasn't for that event alone, I don't know if I would be where I am today, let alone writing a book about eighteen wealth principles. I feel so much gratitude to that friend. Reading that very first book has helped me accomplish so much.

When he refused me money but gifted me the book, I began to develop as a person for the first time in my life. I'm so grateful for that gift that never stops giving to me.

THE EASE OF SHOWING GRATITUDE

It is so easy to show how grateful we are, whether that takes the form of a tip when we are out at a restaurant, or a verbal expression of gratitude. It can be a willingness to help others to not only pay back someone's kindness, but also to show how grateful we can be. Showing gratitude can be as small as a heartfelt handwritten letter or a phone call, or it can be as significant as rewarding a coworker with a trip for their dedication and hard work. Gratitude can take many forms, but it can be effortless. It only takes a second to say "thank you" and mean it.

THE GRATITUDE EFFECT

In positive psychology research, gratitude connects with greater happiness. People feel more positive emotions, enjoy good experiences, improve their health, deal with adversity, and build strong relationships. The more I researched gratitude, the more I realized how powerful it could be in shifting my life in the most positive ways.

In 2013, the journal *Personality and Individual Differences* reported that grateful people experience fewer aches and pains, and they report feeling healthier than other people.[14] Additional research, not surprisingly, says that grateful people are more likely to take care of

---

14   Patrick L. Hill, Mathias Allemand, and Brent W. Roberts, "Examining the Pathways between Gratitude and Self-Reported Physical Health across Adulthood," *Personality and Individual Differences* 54, (January 2013): 92-96.

their health, exercise more often, and get regular medical checkups.[15] The health research around gratitude made total sense to me, and I began noticing how I felt physically in the weeks and months after I began consistently practicing gratitude exercises. Besides feeling physically stronger, I noticed that I felt mentally stronger too.

Robert A. Emmons, PhD, a leading gratitude researcher, has conducted multiple studies on the link between gratitude and well-being. His research confirms that gratitude effectively increases happiness and reduces depression.[16]

When you intentionally show gratitude, you get intentional results.

GRATITUDE IN BUSINESS

The more I practiced gratitude regularly, made it a daily habit, and dove deeper into the gratitude philosophies of other successful people, I realized what a hidden tool it could be in business. Consider two simple facts when it comes to gratitude in your professional life.

First, a 2014 study published in the *Journal of Applied Sports Psychology* found that gratitude increased athletes' self-esteem, which is essential for high performance.[17] Second, other studies have shown that gratitude reduces social comparisons. Rather than becoming resentful toward people who have more money or better jobs—

---

15 Antique Nguyen, "5 Reasons Why Practicing Gratitude is Important in Healthcare," PreCheck Blog, October 11, 2017, https://www.precheck.com/blog/5-reasons-why-practicing-gratitude-important-healthcare.
16 Robert Emmons, "Why Gratitude Is Good," *Greater Good*, November 16, 2010.
17 Lung Hung Chen and Chia-Huei Wu, "Gratitude Enhances Change in Athletes' Self-Esteem: The Moderating Role of Trust in Coach," *Journal of Applied Sports Psychology* 26, no. 3 (2014): 349-362.

which is a significant factor in reduced self-esteem—grateful people can appreciate others' accomplishments.[18]

Working in sales and having to establish a close network of people to help bring my sizeable real estate projects together, I understand the power of making people want to work with you. Acknowledging the contributions of others leads to new opportunities, which are critical to exponential success. Something as simple as a "thank you" shows appreciation and good manners, and can help you win new friends, according to a 2014 study published in the journal *Emotion*.[19] The study found that thanking new acquaintances makes them more likely to seek an ongoing relationship; this includes acknowledging a stranger for holding the door or writing a quick "thank you" note to a coworker.

SWITCH ON YOUR GRATITUDE MINDSET

The first step to switching on your gratitude mindset is to start internally and feel gratitude for yourself, your gifts, and what you have accomplished. Being grateful internally is very challenging because it can often make us feel selfish or egotistical. It is an odd feeling to appreciate yourself and your gifts.

No matter how insignificant, there are plenty of aspects of our daily lives that we can show gratitude toward: a beautiful sunny day, a stress-free drive to work, a happy barista at our favorite coffee shop, or getting a discount on a meal.

---

18   Emmons, op. cit.

19   Lisa Williams and Monica Bartlett, "Warm Thanks: Gratitude Expression Facilitates Social Affiliation in New Relationships Via Perceived Warmth," *Emotion* 15, no. 1 (August 2014).

EXERCISE: "GRATITUDE PRACTICE"

Choose a time at the end of each day to spend ten minutes practicing gratitude. It is essential to do this at the end of the day so you can reflect on the day, experience the gratitude, and go to sleep with these thoughts that can seep into your subconscious.

1. Spend the time thinking about your day, the events, your feelings toward the experiences, and what tomorrow holds for you.

2. Begin by focusing on small things that you can be thankful for, like finding a good parking spot at the grocery store, being able to enjoy a cup of coffee in the morning, someone holding the door open for you, or even that you went to the gym and worked out.

3. As you become aware of all the little things you are grateful for, start to verbalize them. For example, "I am grateful for the person who showed me kindness when holding the door open for me. I am grateful that person saw me as deserving of kindness. I am grateful that I had the willpower to go to the gym today and honor my health and body. I am grateful for the energy to work out and thankful that I am focusing on my health so I can live my best life."

4. Next, spend time focusing on bigger things you are grateful to have in your life: a special relationship, a major business deal, the chance to travel, a positive health diagnosis, your children, or a new opportunity.

5. As you become aware of all the significant things you are grateful for, start to verbalize them: "I am grateful for my significant other and how I can express love and receive love from this person unconditionally. I am thankful that

this person sees the best in me so I can also see the best in me. I am grateful for this business deal and how rewarding it feels to be able to provide new opportunities for my company, coworkers, and clients. I'm thankful that my coworkers share my vision and help me lead them so that we can all prosper together."

6. Finally, review your gratitude and ask the universe to acknowledge your appreciation for both small and big things. Spend a few moments thinking about how you feel after expressing what you are grateful for that day.

When you practice the principle of being grateful every day, whether you reflect privately during meditation or you're expressing personal thanks to those who have shown you kindness or have helped you in some way, the universe will give you more things to be thankful for in return. The universe will recognize that you are sincerely grateful for what life has given you, whether you are rich or poor, and will continue to provide you with good things to be grateful for. When we realize in our lives everything we can be grateful for, our bodies fill with peace, contentment, and happiness for what we already have. We stop needing what we don't have and become satisfied with the things in our lives. When we practice gratitude, we can let go and relax with what we already have. We can go about our days in a calm, grateful, happy mood. The universe recognizes those positive feelings radiating from us and brings more of those feelings into our lives, which will continue to allow us to feel grateful. The basic principle is: be thankful for all the things you have in life, no matter how big or small, and be open to receiving and being grateful.

Without conscious gratitude, I'd still be living on a beach.

—

HAVE IDEAS SO MASSIVE OTHERS GET UNCOMFORTABLE

*The mind is its own place, and in itself can
make a heaven of hell, a hell of heaven.*

—John Milton

Did this journey from homeless to billionaire happen because I got very good at goal-setting and meditation? No. If that were true, we would have a world full of billionaires. Massive success comes from extraordinary discipline, dedication, and the power of bigger thinking. To obtain massive success, you must have and execute large ideas.

Thinking bigger and actualizing concepts are not skills that we are born with. They require exercise.

One of the keys to thinking bigger is to incorporate as many success principles as possible as you dream up your inspired ideas. When you are inspired, your subconscious is feeding your thoughts, which is why you must act on inspired ideas right away, before your subconscious stops feeding you the inspiration. Taking action is the first step to making your ideas grow bigger and bigger.

The second thing you need to focus on when you get a "big idea" is how you can make it more significant and more impactful. Don't focus on how you are going to do it. Don't focus on the cost of the idea or the criticism you might face. So, don't let the naysayers stop you when you get an inspired idea; instead, let your mind go and think about the concept in the grandest sense. Make it so grand that, when you describe it, people get uncomfortable.

CASE STUDY: THINKING BIGGER

In 2006, Blake Mycoskie formed a company that designs and sells shoes, eyewear, coffee, apparel, and handbags.

Here is a breakdown:

- In 2006, while on vacation in Argentina, Mycoskie noticed local polo players wearing alpargatas, a simple canvas slip-on shoe that he began to wear himself (and which became the prototype for the shoe line).

- Mycoskie said that when doing volunteer work in the outskirts of Buenos Aires, he noticed that many of the children were running through the streets with no shoes.

- Mycoskie was grateful to be able to afford shoes when others could not and was passionate about solving a problem—those barefoot children. Being grateful and loving is a powerful combination.

- His inspired idea was to develop a type of alpargata for the North American market, with the goal to provide a new pair of shoes free of charge to the youth of Argentina and other developing nations for every pair sold.

- Mycoskie sought the mentorship of Bill Gates, who encouraged him by confirming that a lack of shoes in Argentina was a major contributor to diseases in children.

- Mycoskie, inspired by his idea, took immediate action by selling his online driver education company for $500,000 to finance his shoe company. He initially commissioned Argentine shoe manufacturers to make 250 pairs of shoes. Sales officially began in May 2006. He had no experience in the shoe industry, so this was a significant risk, but he took it.

- The company name is derived from the word "tomorrow," and evolved from the original concept, "Shoes for Tomorrow Project." TOMS Shoes was born. He started the company with the positive emotions of love and gratitude, wanting to make a real difference.

- After an article ran in the *Los Angeles Times*, the company received orders for nine times the available stock online, and ten thousand pairs sold in the first year. The first batch of ten thousand free shoes went to Argentine children in October 2006.

- His first year was so successful that Mycoskie expanded on his inspired idea. In 2007, the company launched its annual "One Day Without Shoes" event, which encourages people to go shoeless for the day to raise awareness about the impact shoes can have on a child's life. The event has had corporate sponsors such as AOL, Flickr, and the Discovery Channel.

- By 2012, TOMS had provided more than two million pairs of new shoes to children in developing countries around the world.

- In June 2014, Mycoskie set a clear goal to sell part of his stake in the company to help it grow faster and meet the company's long-term goals. Bain Capital immediately acquired it.

- Mycoskie's wealth following the deal was estimated at $300 million; he retained half-ownership of TOMS, as well as his role as "Chief Shoe Giver."

- Mycoskie said he would use half of the proceeds from the sale to start a new fund to support socially-minded entrepreneurship, and Bain would match his investment and continue the company's one-for-one policy.

The point of this example is that TOMS was valued at more than $600 million only six years after Mycoskie's inspired idea surfaced. One for One became an impact model that many businesses have now adopted.

Mycoskie's idea became a massive success for three reasons:

1. He used mentorship (Bill Gates) to add fuel to his idea and make it even more significant.

2. He took immediate action by investing $500,000 to produce the first 250 pairs of shoes.

3. He continued to add to the idea and push its growth by thinking bigger and bigger (charity and investment).

The shoes were not the big idea; he imitated shoes that already existed in Argentina and brought them to North America. The big idea was trying to solve the problem of children without shoes using a successful business.

His big idea continues to get bigger. When TOMS sells a pair of shoes, a new pair of shoes goes to an impoverished child. When TOMS sells eyewear, part of the profit is used to save or restore eyesight for people in developing countries. The company launched TOMS Roasting Co. in 2014, and with each purchase of TOMS Roasting Co. coffee, the company works with other organizations called "giving partners" to provide 140 liters of clean water, equal to a one-week supply, to a person in need. In 2015, TOMS Bag Collection was launched to fund advancements in maternal health. Purchases of TOMS Bags help provide training for skilled birth attendants and distribution of birth kits containing items that help women practice safe childbirth.

Do you believe that Blake Mycoskie's fantastic company resulted from one inspired idea? No. Mycoskie had an initial plan for a shoe company that gave back, which was indulging one of his passionate missions. He started with a singular idea and then applied various success principles discussed in this book. I have a lot of respect for TOMS and what it has done. It is a perfect example of how thinking bigger leads to massive success—and how massive success allows us to improve the lives of those around us.

You can create unlimited opportunities in business and life by training your mind to think bigger. The initial idea can be small, but how you continue to think about it must be massive. I started with wanting to improve my real estate clients' experience during meetings to then creating another business in the coffee shop market.

FAMOUS COFFEE

In the real estate industry, when clients come to meet with developers, coffee and light fare are offered. We want our clients focused and paying attention to our presentations, not thinking about being hungry or thirsty.

One day, someone noticed that our competitors always served their customers mediocre takeout coffee or cheap instant coffee that you can buy at any convenience store. This observation generated an inspired idea.

I immediately visualized how much better the experience would be to have a fantastic coffee shop in our building that always had fresh, delicious coffee and tasty treats that our clients could enjoy. The key now was taking immediate action. We created the first coffee shop in a section of one of our development offices, and we even established our own brand, buying the beans from a Thai plantation famous for its quality and taste. Upon entering our building on the way to a meeting, clients would first experience the coffee shop. Soon enough clients started to come back to our building just for a cup of coffee, a pastry, or a snack. We began getting great reviews of our service, coffee, and food. Eventually, we expanded locally and now have three successful branches.

The big idea to create a coffee shop in our headquarters was to give our clients a special feeling when they came for meetings. However, the idea grew bigger and bigger and then evolved into a franchise. I could have stopped at the one shop, but I kept thinking about how I could make it even better.

Initially, I called the coffee shops Green Mountain, referring to the green region in Thailand that supplied the beans. I decided to rename the coffee shop, because, in one of my thinking sessions, it occurred to me that the right name would evoke the feeling that I wanted people to experience. I decided to rename the coffee shops Famous. Famous is a pretty simple word that people could remember, and I thought customers would enjoy using it. They would say, "Let's meet at Famous," or "I'm at Famous." There is a good feeling associated with the word. When asked, "Where are you going for coffee today?" it's hard not to smile when you say, "I'm going to Famous." It's a single word with positive connotations, and it sounds special, like a place you'd go to meet celebrities. You may just be going for a cup of coffee, but you'll leave feeling great because of the experience. When the name Famous came to mind, I instantly knew that it was going to turn out great. Now all I hear is how much clients enjoy getting Famous.

Others will not see your vision, because it is not their job to do so. It is your job to bring the vision into reality.

CASE STUDY: ACTING QUICKLY ON BIG IDEAS

In 2011, two men got into a discussion at a party about how frustrated they were with the cost of razor blades. They came up with an inspired idea called Dollar Shave Club. What made founders Mark Levine and Michael Dubin so successful was how quickly they acted on their idea. With their own money and investments from start-up incubator Science Inc., they started operations in January 2011 and launched their website ninety days later.

The membership service first launched March 6, 2012, via a YouTube video that went viral, crashing the company's server in the first hour. Once Dubin got the server working, he enlisted a team of friends and contractors to help fulfill the twelve thousand orders that arrived in the first forty-eight hours after launching the video. Even when problems struck the fledgling company, the founders had a clear vision and acted quickly to make the idea happen. Since its launch, the company has acquired 3.2 million subscribers.

The moral of this story is that there is no idea too small to make massive.

THERE IS ALWAYS AN EASIER WAY

I have found that when trying to launch a new idea, especially in business, it can feel too hard. When something is hard, that makes it easy to want to give up. Big ideas can feel hard to execute, which is why I always look for the easiest way to accomplish the big idea. I was born with the desire to do things my way and whenever possible I looked for the simplest way to get things accomplished.

When I was about fourteen, just before I dropped out of high school, I took a sales job during the holiday season. I went door to door, selling boxes of traditional Swedish chocolate cookies called Chokladbollar. The goal was to sell a box to every door I knocked on. It was cold calling sales during the physically cold winter. Each box cost about $30, and I was hearing no, after no, after no.

I thought of trying to sell each cookie individually instead of a whole box. I figured it had to be easier than trying to sell an entire box at a time, and my boss never said I couldn't just sell one cookie at a time. Now, when people opened the door, I would say, "I have a box of Chokladbollar, you can choose one for fifty cents." I found that tactic so much easier because people were willing to buy one or two cookies at a time. This led to more people buying an entire box at a time because they would realize it was cheaper to buy a whole box than just a few cookies. Eventually, I was selling box after box of them. This technique led me to be the best salesperson on the twelve-person team.

There is a solution to every problem, and every challenge allows us to grow stronger and learn things that will only help us to have an easier time in the future. I could have easily given up when I couldn't sell a single box of cookies, but eventually, I relaxed and let the inspired idea come to me. It was because I was so young at the time, and, as we discussed earlier, when we are younger our minds are more creative because the reality of the world has yet to set in. We believe without fear or worry and allow a new range of inspired ideas to penetrate our minds and give us the answers we seek.

Whatever idea comes flashing through your mind, make sure you take the time to write down that idea before you forget it, even if you have to keep a journal next to your nightstand for when ideas come to you in the night or even through dreams. Then, once you have this new idea written down, list what immediate actions you could take to see that new idea become a reality. It could be making a simple call to someone who could help you, or to someone who could provide information. You might need to do a little research to determine what actions are needed. Find the answers to what will make this idea a reality. It's in the process of seeking solutions that you'll find the opportunity waiting for you—the possibility that will lead to your success.

BIG IDEAS: A NUMBERS GAME

Many years later, removed from living on the beach and finding success in real estate, I found myself considering opening up a health and fitness club. It was a big idea, not only in the scope of work it entailed, but also because I had no experience in the fitness arena. This was a big risk for me. I just had a dream that inspired me to go for it. This big idea paid off and became a successful business.

Not all of my big ideas were so rewarding. I invested a significant amount of time and money on fish! I bought Phuket Fishing Park after my first real estate company went bankrupt. I took over a lake with borrowed money and imported huge freshwater fish from different countries into the lake. I built huts for fisherman and supplied all the fishing gear for them to use in the park. A relaxing place to fish without any worries! I was sure that the fishing park would be a success.

Then reality hit. Maintenance. Dead fish. Gardening. Repairs. Problematic staff. It turned out to be much more work than I anticipated, with minimal return on my investment. This big idea sank quickly.

On another occasion, an Australian superannuation funds company approached me to participate in investing abroad. Superannuation is a pension system. This felt like a great way to invest money, do good, and expand my business portfolio. I would be helping Australian clients using their superannuation funds to invest abroad. I knew how to invest, so this felt like a good risk to take. Then I discovered that the Australian broker who had the license to operate this business was a complete drunk and untrustworthy. After investing a significant amount of money in the marketing materials and website, I was forced to abandon the partnership. With so many Australians visiting Thailand at that time, I was happy to take the risk, believing it would pay off. Looking back, I am happy it did not turn into a business.

I have big ideas all the time. I take action and assume the risk. So far, I've had thirteen investments of time and money that failed and nineteen businesses that succeeded. Thinking big and acting on those ideas is a huge part of that success.

TO THINK BIG, START SMALL

Exercise your mind like a muscle to strengthen it and allow yourself to reach for bigger goals. It will take time and practice using the principles in this book to make it a habit. Remember, a single thought must overcome significant obstacles, setbacks, problems, and difficulties before it can realize its full potential. For an idea to grow big and expand, you must accept the harsh realities of life and respond by adjusting where needed but never shrinking. To think big is to do big.

PRINCIPLE #9

—

BE PASSIONATE

Anything that gets your blood racing
is probably worth doing.

—Hunter S. Thompson

It is essential to find out what you love to do—your passion. When you find it, you will enjoy working on it, and this invariably leads to success. For instance, I have always dreamed of living in paradise. I have worked hard to create my haven in Phuket.

It was in Phuket that I discovered my passion, which was life changing, considering only a year prior I was wondering if I would even live past eighteen. I was on a motorbike, handing out brochures for a real estate company. On this particular day, I handed a brochure to a gentleman who was visiting Phuket for business and who was on his way to the airport in a few hours to fly home. He was interested in seeing one of the properties, but only if we could show it to him right away, so he did not miss his plane. I took him immediately to the sales office to get an agent to take him on tour. There was no one at the office; they were all already out on tours. The gentleman stated he would not be able to wait for them to return. I had an inspired thought.

"Well sir, I have a motorbike only, but I would be happy to take you to see the property. You'd have to ride on the motorbike with me, but I can get you there before you have to leave for the airport." Surprisingly, he agreed.

I only knew the location of one of the properties, so I drove him to this location. I spent an hour in total with him explaining the area and showing him the property. When we returned to the office, he said he wanted to buy it. My manager couldn't believe it. How did I close a sale in an hour, on a motorbike, with no sales training? Spending an hour together, I was able to gain his trust. I formed a connection, and he bought it! That was the first time in my life I felt proud of something I had done. It felt great to engage with someone, understand what they were searching for, and be able to connect them with what they wanted. I wanted more opportunities to feel like this. I got them when my manager promoted me to sales. I left my brochures behind for good.

I now own health clubs, coffee shops, a gasoline station, and a spa, plus fifteen other companies within the real estate industry. Friends and family members all have asked me the same question:

"Andres, you talk a lot about having a passion for what you do, but do you have passion for all those different companies that you have created?"

My answer is no. I do not have a deep passion for all these businesses, but I do have a burning passion for creating companies and turning ideas into successful operations. I have a great love for making them profitable and successful.

My passion for and love of being a developer comes from the magic of having an idea that becomes a picture in my mind, then an image on paper, then a drawing, then a price to make it happen, and finally seeing my very own idea and creation in front of my eyes. Everything starts with imagination. All of this creation begins with an image in your head. The satisfaction of converting an idea or dream into actual things that you can feel, see, touch, and smell gives you tremendous joy. It also proves that we are born as creators and we all have the power within us to create anything that comes to mind.

> *Passion is what makes all of the bad stuff worth it.*

FINDING YOUR PASSION

Not being able to recognize your passion can be a problem for those stuck in jobs that they don't enjoy. It's all too easy to fall into a routine that leaves you bored or unfulfilled: you want to make the switch, but you're not sure what to do next.

Finding your passion is easier than you think. By answering these questions honestly, you can work out what to do with the rest of your life:

- What subject could you read five hundred books on without getting bored?

- What could you do for five years straight without getting paid?

- What would you spend your time doing if you had the financial freedom to do anything?

EXERCISE: "DISCOVER YOUR PASSION"

You don't have to be great at something to be passionate about it. If you can't imagine *not* doing something, it's a passion. You can become laser-focused on your goals by making a list of the things you don't want, and then writing the opposite. You can determine your passion in the same way:

1. Start by writing down what you don't like doing.

2. List the jobs or tasks that you loathe.

3. Once you have eliminated these options, your real passion may become more evident.

4. Then create a list of the people you are jealous of by asking the question: "Whom do I envy the most because of the work they do?"

5. List multiple individuals, then look at the work they do and circle the jobs you would like.

6. Eliminate anything on your "jealous" list that is on the list of things you don't like doing.

7. The remaining circled information should provide clues about what can trigger your passion.

COMBINE SKILLS TO DISCOVER YOUR PASSION

Most people have lots of things they are "okay" at doing. According to Oliver Emberton, founder of software start-up Silktide, if you combine your mediocre skills, you'll find your passion.

"Say you're an average artist, with a decent sense of humor," he explains. "You won't have much hope with an art degree, and you can't study 'humor' as a subject. However, you could be an excellent cartoonist."[20]

Emberton argues that the most successful people, the ones who are most passionate about their work, are seldom defined by a single skill.

"They are a fusion of skills, often not even exceptional skills, but they've made their fusion exceptional," he says.

When you consider Steve Jobs, you see that he was not the world's greatest engineer, salesperson, designer, or businessman. He was uniquely good enough at all of these things and wove them together into something far more significant.

Your passions can be endless or always changing, but make sure you discover at least one thing you are passionate about in this world and use it to transform your entire life.

---

20   Oliver Emberton, "How to Find and Master the Mystical Unicorn That Is 'Passion'," *Inc.,* March 27, 2015.

PRINCIPLE #10

—

MASTER YOUR EMOTIONS

Our thoughts, our feelings, our dreams, our ideas, are physical in the universe. That if we dream something, if we picture something, it adds a physical thrust towards realization that we put into the universe.

—Will Smith

Negativity is like the wind: blowing one minute but quickly passing, unable to be stopped. The only way to experience how the wind blows is to let it happen without letting it affect you long-term.

I often get a rolling of the eyes. "Andres, this sounds very silly. When angry, I should think happy thoughts, and everything will get better? Sounds naïve. Negativity is not like the wind." I have heard similar things from new employees as well.

In business, allowing anger, frustration, fear, and other negative feelings to get the best of us can jeopardize big deals, alienate coworkers, lead to poor decisions, and limit opportunity. When you consider that negative emotions can cost you money and profit while limiting your growth, it becomes easier to focus on creating the opposite effects.

The key to turning negative feelings around is first to recognize those feelings and the devastation that can occur by remaining in that state of mind. Then you must switch into focusing on feelings of happiness and love and moving forward.

FINDING A SOURCE FOR POSITIVITY

I embarked on an adventure in Peru that would take me 4,700 meters above sea level to the top of Salcantay in the Andes Mountains and then down into the lost city of Machu Picchu.

We began our trek after just two days of acclimatizing versus the seven days recommended. It was not a smart decision, but we had done several treks at high altitudes, so we thought we could take it. Two group members came down with severe high-altitude sickness and grew critically ill that night after reaching 4,500 meters. That high up on a mountain, with no help for miles, and Mother Nature clearly in control, negativity began to take over the entire group.

Fear and anxiety filled the minds of those who were sick, including thoughts of not making it back down the mountain. Those of us who were not ill were worried, frustrated, and stressed, and we felt helpless in the situation. What started as a once-in-a-lifetime adventure turned into what might be the last big idea for some people on the trip. We had to figure out how we would descend into Machu Picchu with members of our group who were having incredible trouble breathing, much less being able to keep the pace. The weather, the altitude, and the isolation were all pummeling our mindset.

It was on top of that mountain, in the middle of this situation, that I found clarity and the ability to control my emotions, something I struggled with mightily for many years. I looked around at our group. I loved the people I was with very much. We always traveled together. I knew their true spirits. The sky looked like one step from heaven, so incredibly beautiful.

I began to tell myself exactly what I saw to combat the fear and uncertainty that were taking over my mind. I said to myself that I was surrounded by love and beauty and on solid ground. My feet were on the solid ground; the mountain was not shaking or throwing me off the side. The mountain was providing me solid ground for walking down and out of danger. The sky was inspirational, reminding me that we live for moments that take our breath away. The group members loved each other, so our motivations were the same. As I became mindful of my surroundings, I felt my muscles relax.

My breathing regulated because I was surrounded by so much beauty and love. I felt genuine happiness. We made it as a group to the lost city, slowly and carefully, but in high spirits. We learned a big lesson that night: never, ever underestimate Mother Nature, and make sure to prepare well with plenty of sleep, plenty of water, the right clothing, and medical supplies when going on high-altitude treks. A pretty logical lesson!

EMOTIONS ARE POSITIVE AND NEGATIVE

There is an opposite for everything in this life. With love comes hate. With joy comes fear. With success comes failure. For every positive, there is a negative, so it is impossible to go through life without experiencing some form of negativity or pain. The key is not to let it affect your entire life. The more positive your life becomes, the larger the negativity that might arise, but that doesn't mean you should let it stand in the way of great success and wealth.

ACCEPT NEGATIVITY AND PUSH PAST IT

When I was walking through the streets of Stockholm, letting my negative emotions eat at my soul, leading me toward violence and booze, I could not acknowledge the negativity. Therefore, I couldn't focus on the positive. Why? For starters I didn't believe it was possible. Secondly, I was too focused entirely on myself in isolation without any thought to how my actions impacted others. I never once thought about how my dropping out of school, fighting, or drinking affected my family. Had I thought about all the positive things my family gave me, I would have been able to counterbalance all that negativity in my mind. It took years of feeling alone, isolated, unworthy, and desperate for me to realize how much was right around me. My mother giving me permission to "go" was her way of saying she believed in me. Giving me free meals was the noodle lady's way of showing me I was worth it. The signs were there, but I was too filled with self-loathing to see them.

> *New opportunities are allergic to worry, frustration, anger, uncertainty, jealousy, and fear.*

BECOME FEARLESS TO ELIMINATE NEGATIVITY

The mind has more than sixteen thousand thoughts a day. Fear can plague these thoughts with negative emotions.

Engaging in extreme sports (summiting mountains, jumping out of planes, cave diving) forces people to face their fears. Why? Your mind is programmed to support your survival.

CLIMB A MOUNTAIN. LITERALLY.

I love traveling around the world. Not only does it connect me with nature itself, but in doing so, I challenge myself. My most magical moments in life have been sitting on a mountaintop that has taken days to summit. Every muscle burns and your body hurts. You are so exhausted you could lie down and fall asleep for days. You get to feel the quiet, the forever stillness when the first rays of sunlight start shining over the horizon; that moment of bliss when you and nature are one, feeling that deeper connection and having a 360-degree view as far as your eyes can see. Those moments of stillness and awareness allow you to appreciate what it's like to be alive and understand what magical gifts life is offering you.

The mental struggles you endure while summiting a mountain are a constant battle. Your mind tells you a hundred times each step to give up. You fight it, repeating to yourself every step, "Don't ever give up. Take one step at a time!" It's all you have when you want to quit—one step at a time.

I have seen numerous trekkers give up the first day. Mountain climbing has not only been great mental training for myself, but for my colleagues as well. It has taught us that the body is capable of anything, that your mind gives up first, trying to convince you to stop, that you can't do it. It looks for the road easily traveled. Your inner self will be stronger than that voice inside your mind. It's also helped me tremendously in business to realize that you always have those two sides. One is saying no, and the other is saying yes. Follow your yes and never give up.

I have taken many employees to hike mountains, some bigger than others. I have asked them to push their physical limits using the power of their mind. Every time we have descended, they have been happier and more productive.

DEFINITELY JUMP OUT OF A PLANE

I have taken my employees to ski in Japan, climb an active volcano in Indonesia, explore underground caves in Vietnam, jump out of airplanes at four thousand meters with parachutes in Dubai, and climb the highest free-standing mountain in the world. These experiences were worth more than our fears about them.

In fact, in one of my companies, I make it mandatory for my employees to jump out of a plane. I tell them this when we are interviewing them. Most are extremely apprehensive at first and give every excuse why they cannot jump out of a plane. The obvious being "the idea scares me to death, Andres!" I explain to them that fear is the number one thing that holds people back from being wildly successful, and that, in my company, I want to invest in my employees' wild success. I explain that I need employees willing to learn to be fearless. I tell them, "If you can get over your fear of jumping out of a plane, what else is there to be afraid of? Then success is so much easier to achieve." I can honestly report that, of all my companies, the most successful ones are those with the most employees who have jumped out of a plane. There is a direct correlation.

When I first jumped out of a plane it was not because I am an adrenaline junkie—*I* was scared to death—it was because I wanted to stop being afraid of fear so I could lead my fullest life. It was the most life-changing experience for me. It led to so many other opportunities. I am no longer afraid to say "Yes!" when an opportunity comes knocking at my door. I no longer have a fear of falling when I take a leap of faith in business.

Breaking down boundaries makes us unstoppable at work. The experiences that test all your senses, require all your physicality, and get into your soul are the most transformational. The emotional control you master is incredible. You've been to the top and made it back. You've jumped and fallen free without dying. The little things that took you to a negative place before no longer have control over you.

STOP WORRYING

Becoming fearless goes hand-in-hand with cutting worry out of your life. When I started my first business and things started to go south, I began to worry. I worried about everything: sales I needed to keep my business going, being able to pay my employees and bills, losing my house, disappointing my family. Worry feeds fear. My actions became hesitant and laced with anxiety. My thinking became cloudy. Fear was paralyzing me with thoughts of what might happen. I stopped doing the things that had made me successful in the beginning.

I fell back into old habits; I became a spiral of deep negativity, focusing on those worries, and succeeded in bringing those worries into my reality. I lost everything.

When I started my business over, I decided that worrying was bad for profit. It is not an emotion I entertain anymore. I know that it feeds fear too easily. Worrying never gets you off the mountain; action does, one step at a time.

At a certain point, my imagination simply stopped worrying because I knew there was no reason to worry. I knew that what I was working toward would be successful. I have that unwavering confidence in myself because I've failed and proven to myself that I can still succeed despite failure. So, I don't worry anymore. I'm entirely fearless because I know that I will succeed, or, if I fail, I'm going to learn a valuable lesson that will help me in the future.

> *Being a positive person is not a genetic gift; it is a muscle in your mind that you exercise daily. Its strength depends on your conviction to counter negativity with positivity.*

SURROUND GOALS IN POSITIVITY

When a new inspired idea comes to me, I won't lie: I get pretty excited. I like to take action right away, whether that is writing out a detailed list of steps I can take now or getting in touch with the right people who can help me put my idea into action. I don't share my dreams with those who wouldn't understand. I think big and often obtain what most people would consider impossible.

If I were to share my goals with everyone, most would say that I will never be able to do that, or have that, or be that person who has that achievement in life. That's the type of negativity I don't need in my life, especially when a new inspired idea comes to me. My rule of thumb when it comes to my personal goals is that I only share them with people who can help me achieve them. Many times, that includes not sharing my goals with my family. While I love my family, and I know they will always support me in whatever I put my mind to, I don't need them to doubt me for one second. Therefore, I keep my goals close to my heart, and I never let anybody rain on my parade. I want to keep the energy up and growing when it comes to my goals, and that usually means keeping them to myself.

Most people are naysayers who don't understand how powerful these eighteen wealth principles are, how easy they are to use, and how life-changing they are when put into practice. It's always so motivating for me to prove wrong those who doubt that anything I put my mind to is achievable.

I know (not wish) that you can do the same thing. Once you fill your mind with the details of what you want to achieve and then take action to do just that, you'll be able to prove your doubters wrong. Work with me as we prove them all wrong. There is nothing more satisfying. Use any form of outside negativity from others as fuel for the fire that burns inside you; passion propels you toward success. You can do it, no matter how big your goal is, no matter how challenging, regardless of what other people tell you. Deep down inside, believe you will succeed.

PRINCIPLE #11

WAKE UP EXPECTING PROBLEMS

If you do what you've always done, you'll get what you've always gotten.

—Tony Robbins

Big thinkers love big problems and quickly turn them into big opportunities. Challenges are nothing more than puzzles that need to be pieced together with the right resources and ideas. Those who make it a habit of thinking big understand that, while putting the puzzle pieces together, problems will show up at the worst possible time. BIG goals and objectives are only achieved by those with the willpower and resilience to keep on moving forward when everyone else has stopped dead in their tracks because of problems that get in the way. Big thinkers reframe problems into opportunities by twisting their perspective and the perspective of those around them. In other words, they first see the problem for what it is, and then they alter their view of the problem creatively to help them brainstorm better ideas and solutions.

Even though I live a very successful life, a lifestyle most would consider luxurious, I don't live a life that is stress-free. As they say, "More money, more problems," and as an owner of nineteen businesses, as well as being a real estate developer in Thailand's wealthiest location, my life has plenty of stress at any given time. How do I deal with this type of pressure? I wake up every morning thinking that something terrible is about to happen.

Why do I start each morning expecting problems to happen to me? Because I know that problems will always occur, so I don't fight it. I accept that things happen and sometimes I have no control over them.

Now, this principle might surprise you. You might first think that I wake up worried every morning that something terrible is about to happen. But you have learned how I've become fearless and have eliminated worry from my life. Then why do I start each morning expecting problems to happen to me? Because I know that problems will always occur, so I don't fight it. I accept that things happen, and sometimes I have no control over them.

Each new inspired idea, each goal that I write down, will take time, effort, dedication, and any number of things before it becomes a reality, and I can feel that success and see the product of my hard work before me.

Not only do I wake up expecting problems, but I don't mind problems. There's always a solution to any given problem. Problems force you to see things from a different perspective, and no matter the challenge or how unexpected the problem is, there is always a way to overcome whatever problem has popped up. Problem-solving helps you continue learning each day. If you expect problems and make the best out of any unexpected trial, you guarantee yourself the ability to keep learning and gaining the knowledge that is going to help you succeed one day.

If you invoke that feeling of fear and worry as you expect problems, then those feelings will only hinder you from being creative and finding the solutions you need to overcome challenges. Worry and fear will prevent you from gaining the knowledge you'll need to move forward. Expecting problems each morning and loving the challenges life brings can be beneficial, but it doesn't give us an excuse to worry and fear. Remember, you can become fearless and never allow worry to be a problem in your life again. Problems are no more than situations that precede solutions and opportunities.

CHANGING PROBLEMS INTO OPPORTUNITIES

At the risk of sounding like a broken record, I have to talk about mindset again. Everything comes down to solving problems and solving problems comes down to your mindset, or how you turn problems into positive solutions.

To succeed and lead in your field, you not only have to come up with good solutions, you also need to be innovative.

Tina Seelig, the author of *Insight Out: Get Ideas Out of Your Head and Into the World*, has been teaching classes on innovation at Stanford University's engineering school for sixteen years.

"Imagination is envisioning things that don't exist," she says. "Creativity is applying imagination to address a challenge. Innovation is using creativity to generate unique solutions. Entrepreneurship is applying innovations and scaling the ideas by inspiring others."[21]

Reframing a problem helps you see it as an opportunity if your mindset is positive when a problem arises. The key is to remain confident that you will be able to creatively innovate a solution to any problem so that solving problems becomes satisfying to you rather than terrifying. The other key is to systematize how you reframe problems into positive solutions. I respect Seelig's three techniques for doing this: rethink the question, brainstorm bad ideas, and challenge rules.

> *Fear comes from being unprepared.*

RETHINK THE QUESTION

Start by contemplating the question you're asking in the first place. For example, if you're asking, "How do I plan a party to show my customers that I appreciate them without spending too much money?" You're assuming it's a party. Alternatively, if you change your question to: "How can we make our customers' day memorable?" you instantly start thinking of different solutions. Reframing the question allows you to release your focus on the cost and time associated with throwing a party, which could have other problems like budget, location, time, and planning built into it. By refocusing the question, you change how you approach the solution.

---

21 Stephanie Vozza, "Three Ways to Reframe a Problem to Find an Innovative Solution," September 8, 2015, https://www.fastcompany.com/3050265/three-ways-to-reframe-a-problem-to-find-innovative-solution.

BRAINSTORM BAD IDEAS

When facing a problem, it is easy to focus on coming up with only good ideas, but this can limit your problem-solving ability. Instead, it is better to focus on brainstorming bad ideas when trying to come up with creative and innovative solutions—stupid or ridiculous ideas for us to push past obvious answers especially when we remove the pressure of it having to be a "good" idea. Terrible ideas can be re-evaluated, often turning them into something unique and brilliant.

When you face a severe problem, write down as many bad ideas as you can brainstorm in the shortest time. Force yourself not to spend time trying to perfect these ideas; make a list of bad ideas. Later you can brainstorm how to make your bad ideas good ones.

One of the examples Seelig teaches in her class has to do with selling bikinis in Antarctica. A group was asked to make this bad idea a good one. Within five minutes of brainstorming bad ideas, the group came up with a slogan, "Bikini or Die." They reframed a bad idea into an excellent one of taking people who want to get into shape on a trip to Antarctica and putting them through fitness training. By the end of the hard journey, they would be able to fit into their bikinis.

"Selling bikinis in Antarctica sounds like a terrible idea. Within five seconds, when asked to look at it differently, the team came up with a way to transform it into an exciting idea," she says.[22]

CHALLENGE RULES

Another way to positively reframe a problem is to challenge the rules you assume have to be followed. Ask, "What are all of the rules of

---

22   Ibid.

the industry?" Again, start by making a list of the rules you assume must be followed when solving the problem. Then think about what happens if you do the opposite of what the rule dictates; this is hard to do because we are so deeply rooted in rules and assumptions.

"Cirque du Soleil challenged assumptions about what a circus is. Instead of cheap entertainment for kids, they turned it into a high-end event for adults that competes with the theatre or opera," Seelig says.[23]

I love how Southwest Airlines runs its business.

The carrier challenged the rule that airlines had to have fixed seating assignments. By eliminating the practice of assigned seats, Southwest opened up the possibility of having riders line up before each flight so they could choose their seats when boarding the plane. This radically different approach to seating assignments led to more profit for the company, as it was able to charge small fees to have passengers board the plane early and choose their own seats.

USING YOUR TEAM TO SOLVE PROBLEMS

Problem-solving should not be scary since you have ways to think through those problems and creatively solve them. Besides, bringing your team into the problem-solving process is essential.

Whenever a problem arises, I pay close attention to how it happened and analyze the situation to see how to prevent it in the future. Most of the time I gather my executives in for a meeting, and I raise the problem we have encountered in production or any other part of the company. I let them all brainstorm with each other and myself: How could this problem have ever happened? What do we do about it now? How can we learn from it and prevent it in the future?

---

23   Ibid.

Having your employees participate in problem-solving encourages team building. They feel empowered and vital to be involved in some of the decision-making. Most of the time, new and brilliant ideas arise from problems or situations when we are discussing them together as a whole. We find better, quicker, and more productive ways of doing a specific task that created the problem in the first place.

At one point my real estate development company and I were about to launch a new development, a 446-condominium building about five hundred meters from the sea. I was close to signing the purchase agreement and buying the piece of land when another developer launched a beautiful development about two hundred meters away from the seashore. As most of you know, location is often the prime factor in the real estate business.

I gathered all my sales agents and executives that very same day, since I knew we had to decide whether to go ahead and compete with this other development with better proximity to the beach and the same price structures as ours.

We compared the strategic differences and the benefits of our project with our new upcoming competitor. We looked at location, pricing, facilities, and service, and in each they were just a bit better than us. We weren't going to risk a costly and half-sold development after completion. Even though we had already paid a substantial amount to architects, lawyers, and graphic designers, we all decided to drop the development. It would have been too much of a risk to take (even for someone like me who likes to take risks).

Six weeks later, my architect received a phone call from a landowner who needed to sell a block of land. My architect asked me if I could meet him the following day to see the land. I didn't expect much at that time, since scouting for land and visiting different sites is a common thing among us developers. My architect drove us to the same city as the condo development that we recently abandoned, but he did not stop there and continued further toward the sea. We passed by the development site of our competitor and then I got excited. We arrived at our destination. I was now only fifty meters from the beach on a beautiful mountain overlooking the beach with the blue ocean in front of us. The price was reasonable and not much higher than our previously planned development, because the owner needed a quick sale. We finalized a price and settled within the next week.

When great opportunities arise, you better grab them quickly or someone else will do it instead.

We were now in the game again! During the following months, our architects, lawyers, engineers, and graphic designers worked on our new existing development 150 meters away from our competitors' property. We studied their development inside and out, and we aimed (and succeeded) to make ours even better. Today it stands as one of the crown achievements of our company.

We launched our project four months later than our competitor, but sold out our 446-condominium development in six months. Our competitors had only managed to sell a third of their developments at the very same time. We received recognition for Best Investment Project, Best Mix Use Development, and even Best Developer the following year from both the prestigious Thailand Property Awards and the prestigious Asia Pacific Property Awards organization.

If I had not gathered my executives and sales agents that day for decision-making and brainstorming, I might have gone ahead with the initial development and ended up as our competitor did ... left behind—literally. We were all proud to become the leading real estate developer in South Thailand.

HASTY DECISIONS

This experience of working with my team members on the most extensive property development in the history of our company taught me that, when facing a problem or a challenge, it's important not to make a hasty decision. It's better to not decide at all than to make a mistake. When most people have a problem, they want to find and implement a solution so quickly that sometimes they don't take the time to see if that solution is the best fit for that problem. Hasty decisions often lead to more problems. It takes time to do the necessary research to make an inspired decision for solving any problem. Again, it is better to wait and make no choice than to make the wrong decision and pay for it later.

I've discovered through the years that many people are afraid of deciding because they're afraid of making the wrong decision. They are so scared that they never choose to take any action; therefore, they are never able to progress and overcome challenges. They simply become paralyzed, unable to do anything about inevitable problems that life has given them. The problem is that negative thoughts fight to control our minds. Ideas like, "What if I do this and I lose the business?" or, "What if I take this action and I upset my clients?"

It takes time and practice to silence the mind, to cut out all negative thoughts, and to focus instead on the "yes" your brain is trying to tell you—what your inner voice is trying to speak to you. With any problem, silence your mind, think about what solutions you could implement by allowing creativity to flow through you, and don't let any negative thoughts of fear or worry penetrate your healthy mind.

When inspired solutions flash into your mind, take inspired action to solve those problems and gain the knowledge you need to move forward in life.

Every challenge completed is a valuable life lesson. When my first business didn't work out, I learned so much from that experience. I learned what not to do next time. I learned that I needed to keep meditating every day, to keep giving myself goals to accomplish, and to fill my whole body with feelings of love and happiness. Businesswise, I learned that it was more important to gain clients than to impress them with ample office space with fancy computers and several employees. I learned what made a real estate agency appealing to clients and how to truly cater to the people I was trying to bring into my office.

Even after doing several high-altitude hikes previously, that one hike to Machu Picchu taught me that no matter how prepared I might think I am, unexpected problems will arise.

I am always grateful for the problems and challenges that arise in my life, because I know it's merely the universe giving me an opportunity to learn something of great value. Every problem contains a wealth of knowledge. Don't stress about issues, because we all know that they will happen. So, instead of fearing challenges, accept that they are a part of life and begin to expect them. That way when they do occur, you'll be prepared to find a creative solution that will result in your success and increased wealth.

Remember, you can be wealthy just because of what you have learned from the life experiences you've overcome and conquered. You are capable of doing anything, of triumphing over any problem and gaining every bit of knowledge you need to succeed and see your goals accomplished.

PRINCIPLE #12

—

EMBRACE APOLOGY

Respect the old when you are young, help the weak when you are strong, confess when you are wrong, because one day you will be old, weak, and wrong.

—Ang Losang

I carry this quote near and dear to the center of my being. I learned it from a wise Buddhist monk named Ang Losang, whom I had the privilege of spending time with in the high Himalayan Mountains while in Nepal.

I have met many accomplished, successful, and legendary change-makers in the world, and have noticed that they share one trait: great people are not afraid to admit they are wrong, and they make sure not to repeat the same mistakes twice. Great leaders grow in the eyes of their followers, and when they apologize and make sure to do things differently or not at all in the future, this behavior makes their followers see them as strong human beings and leaders who take responsibility for their mistakes and learn from them.

Taking responsibility for our actions boosts our self-esteem and reduces guilt. An apology has the power to humble even the most arrogant people. It takes courage to admit our wrongs and work past our resistance to apologizing, but it leads to a deep sense of self-respect.[24]

I'll never forget when my boss at the telemarketing company yelled at me for making a mistake. I didn't want to lose my job, even though I hated working there. I quickly apologized but inside I was seething. I hadn't done enough wrong to deserve such a dressing down in front of my coworkers. In my mind, he was in the wrong, and my apology was simply the quickest way to end the encounter. He should have apologized to me for yelling, regardless if I had made a mistake or not. I have always remembered how that moment made me feel about the job, my place in the company, and my ability to succeed there. I was not worth the apology.

When I started my own companies, I never wanted to make a mistake and not be willing to admit my wrongs and apologize. I always want the people around me to feel like they are worth my self-reflection and humility.

Many people have issues around apologies, and not all of our thoughts and feelings about apologies line up. Maybe we were forced to apologize as children. Maybe growing up we were made to feel ashamed when we offered an apology.

---

24   Michael Rennier, "The life-changing benefits of a good apology," Aletia.org, July 22, 2018, https://aleteia.org/2018/07/22/the-life-changing-benefits-of-a-good-apology/.

For some people, apologizing feels like admitting we are inadequate—that, rather than having made a mistake, there is something inherently wrong with us. Perhaps you believe that the first apology after an argument is an admission of guilt and responsibility for the entirety of a conflict. Maybe an apology feels like the other person is taking no responsibility for that person's part in the problem.

A well-delivered, appropriately sincere apology will generally avoid all of these issues, and will merely serve to usher in a resolution, reaffirm shared values, and restore positive feelings.

Whenever there has been a misunderstanding between my employees and I, I'm always the first to apologize and say I'm sorry, it's my fault, that I've not been clear enough regarding this situation, event, or rule. Even sometimes when you're not wrong, an apology can change the whole energy in a situation.

I ask the team or group of employees, "How can we make sure that it does not happen again?" I also make sure that I'm clearer and more informative next time this topic or situation arises. I always like to end a meeting discussing a negative event by saying, "Let's learn from this and make sure it doesn't happen again."

Apologizing does not always mean you are wrong and someone else is right. It just means you value your relationship more than your ego.

—**Mark Mathers**

PUT GOOD ENERGY INTO APOLOGIZING

I am not a perfect person, by any means. There are times where I have made a mistake, or an investor is not happy with the results of a development. When this happens, I make sure to meet with that investor as soon as possible and find a way to create the change needed to move forward with a better working relationship. Most of the time I have to be completely honest about what is happening in the development to work with the investor to see positive change happen. Meeting in person restores good energy because it is a lot more personal than a phone call or email. Meeting face to face allows negative energy to change into good energy, and animosity to fade away. I also try to do something a little extra for the investor to help cement the bond between us.

Whenever one of my clients is unhappy about something my business did or did not do, I always make sure to restore our working relationship by going above and beyond. I want to show each client and investor I work with that I'm the best developer in Thailand; I want to show them that my team is a joy to work with on projects. This in turn influences them to continue investing with me and recommend me to their friends as well. I don't settle for mediocre. I make sure every development is done right, that I honor my investors, and that happens by being willing to apologize and make problems right again, and then ensure these particular challenges never happen again.

We are all capable of being humble, of finding creative solutions to challenges, so when you do make a mistake, be willing to admit when you are wrong and do what is necessary to make things right again. There is nothing cowardly about recognizing when you are wrong. It takes a compelling individual to admit fault, do everything possible to fix the wrong, and prevent it from ever happening again. My clients and investors see that powerful individual in me, and so do my many employees. I'm a leader to others and not just those who work for me. I'm a leader in my industry, and all my competitors can see my characteristics and know that, if I am at fault for anything,

I will stick to my word and ensure every business that I own will always be a success, and reasonably accomplished.

Apologizing allows us to discuss what the "rules" should be in the future, especially if a new rule is needed, which is often the case when you didn't hurt the other person intentionally. If you care about the other person and the relationship, and you can avoid the offending behavior in the future, an apology is usually a good idea.

Similar to the law of vibrational giving, apologies should come with positive emotion and no expectation of an apology in return.

Insincere apologies are often a way to avoid guilt. For instance, a public figure writes insensitive tweets and, after taking some heat for them, states, "My comments might have come off as insensitive and ill-timed. For that, I apologize."

This apology was an attempt to avoid responsibility. The apology came across as lame without genuinely addressing the wrong. If that were me, I'd continue to feel sick about it.

BENEFITS OF APOLOGIZING

When we owe someone an apology, it impacts us physically and mentally. We toss and turn in bed at night; we can have a sinking feeling in our chest; we may eat more, or drink more than we should, and even get headaches.

Apologizing affects us not just physically, but mentally. It can lower incidents of depression and anxiety and help renew past relationships. Old grudges create baggage and continue to affect new relationships. Sometimes I've been tempted not to apologize because I think I'll never see the person again and the problem will fade away; this creates inner conflict within me that comes across in negative thinking and self-doubt.

One organization that has shown the positive benefits of learning how to apologize is Alcoholics Anonymous. During AA's support meetings, members learn the twelve steps, which focus on taking a moral inventory and righting past wrongs. The ninth step is about making amends. People in AA have repeatedly said that fearless, honest self-examination of past mistakes has been essential in their recovery.

APOLOGIZING IS A SKILL

Ang Losang, that wise Buddhist monk, talked with me about finding inner peace in the busy world, about opening up to experience pure joy, and about keeping negativity from clouding my judgments and actions. My time with this monk to this day remains one of the most transformative experiences of my entire life. He said, "Respect the old when you are young, help the weak when you are strong, confess when you are wrong, because one day *you* will be old, weak, and wrong."

In both life and business, this is incredible advice. It incorporates so many aspects of the wealth attraction and unlimited opportunity creation principles that I live by and teach. When I review my life, I can see where this advice played out in my benefit. For me, learning to admit my wrongs with the right emotion and sincerity has made a significant difference in my success.

You might remember when the actress Reese Witherspoon was caught on tape being rude to a police officer who suspected her and her husband of drunk driving. When Witherspoon appeared on *Good Morning America*, she said, "We went out to dinner in Atlanta, and we had one too many glasses of wine, and we thought we were fine to drive, and we were not. It's completely unacceptable, and we are so sorry and embarrassed. We know better, and we shouldn't have done that." America forgave her immediately. Why?

Witherspoon's apology follows three simple steps:

First, be honest about the mistake. Take full responsibility and don't try to justify it or explain it away.

Second, drop any pretense that the other person did anything wrong; don't blame others for what happened.

Third, don't let the situation linger. Ask for forgiveness quickly, without worrying too much about how embarrassing it might be.

Developing your apology skills is one of the best ways to continuously attract new opportunities in your life because it keeps you moving forward, not weighed down with baggage, and open to receive back from others. The better you develop those skills, the more wealth you will experience in your business, your relationships, and your own internal experiences.

PRINCIPLE #13

—

FIT BODY. STRONGER MIND.

Take care of your body. It's the only place you have to live in.

—Jim Rohn

As you've no doubt discovered by reading this book, I love staying active. I prioritize it, whether that is going on a hiking adventure, or just going to the gym. I've discovered many benefits from staying active and keeping fit. Life can become so busy that we often put ourselves on the back burner. Staying fit is a practice of self-love that ensures you are being taken care of, both physically and mentally. When you take care of your body with exercise and a good, healthy diet, you are also strengthening your mind, making you more receptive to attracting wealth and new opportunity into your life.

I enjoy mountain climbing, skydiving, bungee jumping, skiing, bodybuilding, and football. I've climbed the Himalaya Mountains, which became an inspiration to name one of my development projects "Grand Himalai." I genuinely believe that the adrenaline and stress of an adventure are better than a thousand peaceful days.

Whenever I go to the gym, lift weights, or do cardio, I often receive creative ideas and the motivation I need to move forward with the goals that I have written down. Since you gain confidence when you work out, you feel stronger and healthier. It's also a great way of relieving stress, anxiety, and worries. People who regularly exercise often enjoy a greater feeling after their workout sessions. Routinely using your body gives you a boost in happiness and higher energy levels. That's why many devoted gym-goers continue coming back for more, because they know the benefits: the great feelings they obtain from working out, and the confidence boost from having a healthy body image.

The good vibes from exercising connect to the endorphins that the body produces when we work out.

Endorphins are connected to your body's reward circuits as well as the activities such as eating and drinking. Endorphins also increase the response to pain and stress, such as exercise. Endorphins help people feel good after their workouts. Some people like me get addicted to these feelings. Just as pharmaceutical drugs can be addicting, so can the feeling that we get from working out—a desirable sense of stress-free happiness and confidence, without the nasty side effects of addiction, of course.

Earlier I explained how my fitness club came into existence. The fitness and health club is filled with state-of-the-art equipment, cardio machines, saunas, steam rooms, and daily classes for fitness, dance, yoga, martial arts, and high-intensity training. I encourage employees to stay healthy and train whenever they have a chance, and even hold morning meetings at the club to unite employees who work in other industries and companies. It's a great way to get the motivation going across all companies. I often hand out free passes, memberships, and exceptional promotions to get employees to start a routine of regular exercises. It's all worth it.

A healthy lifestyle not only changes your body, but it also changes your mind, your attitude, and your mood.

Focusing on the improvement of your physical body forces you to focus on your mind and spirit.

SUCCESSFUL PEOPLE PRIORITIZE EXERCISE

One of my wealth attraction principles talks about mimicking successful people and business models. When I started to push myself farther and farther to achieve the 101 goals I set for myself each year, I researched the habits of other highly successful people. How did they accomplish so much in the same twenty-four-hour period I had to accomplish things? How did they increase their output of great ideas? As with anything, study habits and you will uncover the formula for success.

I've researched the focus placed on exercise by some of the world's most successful people:[25]

- Mark Zuckerberg, founder and CEO of Facebook, works out at least three days per week, usually in the form of

---

25 Andrew Merle, "The Exercise Habits of Ultra-Successful People," October 19, 2017, https://medium.com/@andrewmerle/the-exercise-habits-of-ultra-successful-people-37f770cdbea0.

taking his dog running first thing in the morning. He became one of the world's youngest billionaires.

- Richard Branson, founder of Virgin Group, wakes as early as five o'clock to kite surf, swim, or play tennis. He claims he gets four hours of additional productivity every day by keeping up with his consistent exercise schedule. He owns more than three hundred companies.

- Condoleeza Rice, former US Secretary of State, gets up at 4:30 in the morning to get in forty minutes of cardio, usually on a treadmill or elliptical machine. She has become one of the most important political figures in US history.

- Barack Obama, former President of the United States, exercises for forty-five minutes a day, six days per week. He exercises first thing in the morning, alternating between lifting weights one day and doing cardio the next. He was not only the most powerful man in the world for eight years, but he is also an accomplished father, speaker, and author.

- Mark Cuban, owner of the NBA's Dallas Mavericks, does an hour of cardio per day, six to seven days a week. He does the elliptical and Stairmaster, plays basketball, and takes kickboxing and other aerobic gym classes. He appears on the popular television show *Shark Tank* and has become a worldwide investor in new start-ups.

- Tim Cook, CEO of Apple, wakes at 4:30 and hits the gym several times per week. He also enjoys cycling and rock climbing. Apple continues to be an innovative leader in emerging technology globally.

The more I researched the world's most successful people, the more commonality I discovered. They start their days early, making any form of exercise a priority, and they have lots of variety in their routines. I was fascinated by this but faced a problem. Anyone who knows me understands that I am not a morning person. My internal clock is not wired to wake up early in the morning. So, the thought of exercising before six o'clock is not something that I relish.

John Ratey, MD, a leading expert in the space, wrote a best-selling book on the topic called *Spark: The Revolutionary New Science of Exercise and the Brain*.

In the book, Ratey calls exercise "the single most powerful tool you have to optimize your brain function."[26]

He points out that exercise helps:

- improve learning ability and grow brain cells;

- alleviate stress, anger, anxiety, and depression;

- increase focus, attention, and alertness; and

- reduce the risk of age-related disorders such as Alzheimer's, Parkinson's, and other forms of dementia.

Moreover, he details the best exercise regimen for optimal brain performance:

- At a minimum, we should do some moderate-intensity aerobic activity for thirty minutes at least five days a week. For your aerobic exercise, activities like running, cycling, or swimming are great, but the best type of aerobic activity is whatever you will genuinely be able to build into your lifestyle. If you haven't been active in a while, the best way to begin is to start walking.

---

26   John Rately, *Spark: The Revolutionary New Science of Exercise and the Brain*, (Boston, Massachusetts: Little, Brown and Company 2008).

- It is best to do some form of aerobic activity six days a week, for forty-five minutes to an hour. Make sure not to do the high-intensity days back-to-back to let your body and brain recover.

- Add some form of strength or resistance training to build muscles, strengthen bones, and protect joints.

- Adding in more complex activities will develop skills, challenge the brain, and help you stay agile—for example, rock climbing, martial arts, gymnastics, dance, yoga, Pilates, or balance drills. Racket sports are especially great because they simultaneously tax the cardiovascular system and the brain. The combination of challenging the mind and body has a more significant positive impact than aerobic exercise alone.

- Consider joining an exercise group to get going and keep you on track. Social interaction is excellent for health, reduces stress, and boosts motivation.

He advises doing something almost every day but keeping your exercise program flexible and trying new things. He emphasizes doing complex activities like martial arts, yoga, gymnastics, or rock climbing. He does not emphasize exercising early in the morning. For me, this made all the difference, and I started scheduling fitness breaks into my daytime hours, which always leaves me mentally supercharged. As someone who suffered from depression for many years, I have seen the remarkable brain-positive, mood-regulating effects of regular exercise. The fitter I am, the stronger my mental acuity and outlook are. There is no doubt that activity is incredibly powerful for both the mind and body.

We're awake for at least sixteen hours each day. Spending just one of those hours (or even half an hour) exercising will be the most important thing you do all day!

MAKING EXERCISE WORK FOR YOU

Exercise doesn't need to be going to a class or lifting weights at the gym. It can be joining a team sport and attending practices and games each week. If you're not a big fan of sports, perhaps there is a beautiful garden on your way home from work. Take the time to stop by the park, and walk around the gardens for thirty minutes, allowing you to decompress from the day and let all the stress leave your body before you make it home to your family. Maybe you've always wanted to be a yoga teacher. By taking steps to achieve this dream, you're not only exercising but dedicating your time to both being physically active and fulfilling a business dream. Make exercising work for you, so that when you take the time out of your day to do something physical that will benefit you, it is also helping you achieve what you want, whether that is more friends, your black belt in Taekwondo, or a certification to lead an exercise class.

There are countless benefits to exercising. Once you get in the habit of being more active, exercising both your body and mind, you'll find that obtaining your goals is easier. You're more prepared for life's challenges, for focusing your mind on finding creative solutions, and you'll have the energy and determination already built into your body to withstand life's trials that arise when you journey toward success. You'll envision your goals with more clarity and be able to see yourself succeeding now, wrapped in all those positive feelings we get from being successful. You'll be able to physically work harder and longer to achieve those goals faster because you've built up stamina from exercising, and, on a biological level, you're releasing many feel-good hormones that are going to propel you further.

No matter what kind of exercise or physical activity you decide to start, my best advice is never to stop or give up. Life will always be busy. There is never a perfect time to start something new. It all comes down to just doing it, to making it a priority in your life, and staying in the habit of practicing self-love, of putting yourself first, if only to make sure you stay healthy and happy. Life will continue to change around you, but never cut exercise from your life to save a little bit of time in your day. Remember, you don't have to go to the gym every day. A simple walk home will be enough to keep you on the path of improving yourself and succeeding in life.

PRINCIPLE #14
—
PAY MORE, GIVE MORE, KEEP MORE

We rise by lifting others.

—Robert G. Ingersoll

Rich Dad Poor Dad author Robert Kiyosaki[27] says, "Rich is measured in money and wealth is measured in time. Most people focus on getting rich rather than becoming wealthy."

I agree.

One of the "secrets" you don't hear too much about when it comes to wealth attraction is how to keep wealth once you have it. In both life and business, wealth is not only how much money you

---

27   Robert Kiyosaki, *Rich Dad Poor Dad*, (First Borders Edition: 2009).

have, but it is also how loyal and committed your teams are, and how much time you have to spend on your passions outside of business. I learned to measure my wealth in terms of happy teams, free time, and intangible benefits.

After running dozens of successful businesses, I teach the concept of "Pay More, Give More, Keep More."

- *Pay more* than you are expected to when compensating your team and vendors, because they will pay more attention to detail, which your clients will deem valuable.

- *Give more* personal, non-monetary compensation to your team, vendors, and clients.

- *Keep more* time for yourself by managing your team, vendors, and clients from afar.

PAY MORE

Simply put, if you want the very best for your business, then you must make sure that you are working with the best. Working with the best requires you to pay them more.

Our largest investor, who has purchased more than 136 properties, once told us he chose us after visiting with our competitors. His reason was simple: "Your organization and employees pay that extra attention to detail, which made me certain that you were the right choice for me."

If a business is always looking to maximize profit, it focuses on cutting expenses whenever possible—including employees' wages. The truth is that most companies pay employees as little as they can get away with. That's the perfect way to encourage workers who will, in turn, provide as little effort as they can get away with. This is a backward way of thinking about compensation. A profit-first mentality of paying the lowest-possible wages ultimately cripples employee performance and engagement and damages your bottom line.

RESULTS OF PAYING MORE

When employees and vendors are not worried about money, they focus on details, and getting the details right. This saves money overall and raises client satisfaction. Here are the benefits of paying more:[28]

- Great people don't work for garbage wages. They're smart, and they know their worth; that's part of what makes them exceptional. If you fish at the bottom of the barrel, that's what you'll catch.

- If you want people to perform at higher levels, set the bar higher. You can't excite top performers when you have low expectations. If you pay employees generously, then you can expect more from them and hold them to a higher standard. They will also expect more from themselves.

- Research shows that happy employees are 12 percent more productive than their less-than-enthused counterparts.

- Paying more keeps your best people more loyal.

- Consumers love doing business with companies that treat their people well. When you interact with employees who don't care about their jobs, it's noticeable and unpleasant.

---

28   Michal Addady, "Study: Being Happy at Work Really Makes You More Productive," *Fortune*, October 29, 2015, http://fortune.com/2015/10/29/happy-productivity-work/.

LEARNING BY PAYING LESS

On one of my first big development projects, I negotiated very strictly and landed the lowest contractor prices around. The problems started when the architects that I hired were not able to produce drawings and plans on schedule. They did not have enough staff or skilled workers such as engineers based on the budget I had negotiated with them. They ended up outsourcing the job, which caused more delays and challenges. Because they were making very little on the job, the architects, designers, and everyone else I employed produced low-quality work using cheap materials. This ended up costing me much more in the long run in repairs to their work, having to tear it down, and starting all over again.

By negotiating for the lowest rates, I caused everyone to cut corners because they had to be conscious of maintaining a profit for themselves.

CAN YOU AFFORD TO PAY MORE?

Business myth: Small companies can't afford to hire the best because they are focused on staying out of debt and boosting profit.

Business fact: This is running a business with a scarcity mentality. Hire what you can afford and you get results you can afford. By changing your mindset to one of abundance, you can start taking steps to hire the best and in turn get the best results, which will produce more revenue and more satisfied customers, not to mention more free time for you. Perhaps you can't afford to pay too much more when first starting your business—this is where giving more helps tremendously.

GIVE MORE

"Give more" means you give more than just money to your employees to spur higher levels of job satisfaction. "Give more" can be benefits, bonuses, education, incentives, responsibility, or shared ownership—anything that has value to employees and is not related to their salary.

People are motivated by money only up to a certain point. I knew this to be true given all my false starts in life. We, as a species, desire the intangible things money can't provide, like feeling valued, appreciated, and recognized. This is why we should give more.

I've had the most exceptional people in the industry join my team not only for the premium wages or the better benefits, but because we provide them with a greater team environment, inspiration to be better, education to become a happier and more successful person, and higher chances of growth. If you want the best in the business working for you, make sure you can offer them something that will set you apart from your competitors. They need to see that working with you is their best option in the industry and personally.

By getting to know your employees, you will know how to create "give more" situations that motivate them beyond money and don't cost you very much. You can implement one, two, or more nonmonetary benefits to an employee's package that add tremendous value. Things like:

- flexible schedules,

- paid time off for personal development or family,

- cross training,

- online class tuition,

- workplace wellness programs,

- motivational seminars,

- structured bonus programs, and/or

- shares in the company.

GIVE MORE FAITH, TRUST, AND RUNWAY

Employees want to feel empowered; your faith in their decision-making ability can be more valuable than money in many respects. One of the ways to build that faith is to allow them to work in jobs they were not originally hired for; it shows you have faith that they can succeed with new things. By giving employees more responsibility to make decisions without fear of making a mistake, you build trust. By putting employees in charge of solving problems, you show them that they have the runway to be a leader. These are incredibly powerful ways to create loyal employees who will have your company's best interests at the forefront.

When developing a new business, I usually don't have any managers right away. I allow employees to work as a team to achieve success with me as their leader, setting an example of how I expect the business to run. It's a very empowering business model that I use with every one of my companies.

Once I assemble my team, and I've had time to review everyone's performance, I choose the one or two individuals who demonstrate keen leadership skills and can work hard under pressure and encourage those around them to be successful. I also pick those whom I can trust and believe in the most, people I know will help motivate the entire team to keep pressing forward. It's hard to tell how someone will perform just based on a résumé, but when you put employees in real work situations, then you can see how they will perform.

I never want one of my managers to think they are the enemy because they are new to the business instead of having previous experience working with that particular team. When it comes to working with the best, you must hire those you already know are top people from within your own company; doing this gives more faith, trust, and runway to these critical employees going into important managerial roles. Faith, trust, and runway are incredibly rewarding.

Applying this strategy has given me the very best employees in the industry, from sales superstars to the most talented marketing executives, accountants, financial people, and trainers. Paying an employee more and providing them more reasons to be inspired and loyal is an incredible combination.

We pay a heavy price—both personally and collectively—when we treat employee engagement and profitability as separate.

—Arianna Huffington

FILL EMPLOYEE EXPERIENCES WITH PURPOSE

When you create employee experiences that are rooted in a shared purpose, you tap into what is called a "North Star." Having a shared North Star, or guiding passionate principles, is critical for creating employee engagement.[29] In my companies, I make it a point to hire people who are more open to trying new things; this is not always the case when I hire employees, but it is a heavy consideration. My staff includes many millennials, who generationally have a height-

---

29   Charlie Brown, "Keys to Earning Sustained Loyality From Your Employees," June 21, 2018, ChiefExecutive.com, https://chiefexecutive.net/keys-to-earning-sustained-loyalty-from-your-employees/.

ened desire to connect to a bigger-than-profit purpose behind their work. They naturally crave the opportunity to contribute to their potential and prefer performance rewards that tap their true motivations. Purpose has become the most critical market differentiator of our time—but it's also your most valuable talent recruitment and retention tool.

One of my favorite examples of this is Southwest Airlines. For more than forty years, Southwest has shared company profits with its workforce. Each week, CEO Gary Kelly publicly praises employees who've gone the extra mile (no pun intended) to exemplify great customer service. The airline's in-flight magazine, *Southwest Spirit*, features employees who go above and beyond, while down-to-earth videos shared internally further capture the company's passion. Purpose was never a marketing campaign for the airline. It's the North Star guiding everyday decisions and behavior across the workforce. The company operationalized its purpose throughout its culture by tying exceptional service to profit. Equally important, it used the power of storytelling to reward high performers, embedding the purpose across the employee journey. I firmly believe in the principle of giving more.

When we design engagement—strategies grounded in purpose and aligned to employees' underlying aspirations—productive, loyal, high-performing teams can emerge.

KEEP MORE

One of the critical factors in keeping the wealth you attract in your life is to have enough time to reflect on it, enjoy it, and continue the practices that made the wealth possible.

Reflecting on your wealth is very important because it helps you feel gratitude toward it, determine how to best use it, and reflect on the things you need to do to maintain it. Reflection requires thinking time, or Principle 4.

Enjoying your wealth, both monetary and intangible, also requires time—free time. Free time means that you can physically and mentally detach from your responsibilities. This allows you to put real time into enjoying family, friends, experiences, and self-evolution without the mental ties to your business; this is key to long-term success.

Continuing the practices that made you wealthy is also paramount. When I let my business get the best of me (generally by micromanaging), I stop making time to think, set goals, visualize, stay physically active, and take inspired action. These are all the things that helped me attract wealth and opportunity in the first place.

If you are not able to keep more of your time away from being actively engaged in your business, then you will always be chasing wealth, as opposed to attracting it. It is important to place as high a priority on keeping more of your time free as it is in attracting and retaining the best employees. Keeping more time free requires that you not micromanage your well-paid teams.

MICROMANAGING STEALS YOUR TIME

Micromanaging is one of the most damaging habits a leader, entrepreneur, or business executive can have. It goes against the principles of giving more and keeping more. Teams get bogged down going through laborious procedures, and worse is the environment it generates. Groups that adapt to a micromanagement style are either quietly rebellious or hapless, unable to make any independent decisions. Compensation matters less and less in this downward spiral.[30]

Micromanaging leaves you continually putting out fires, rather than focused on the tasks that only you can perform.

Why micromanage, especially when it is counterproductive to the "Pay More, Give More, Keep More" strategy? The reason for micromanaging ranges from lack of trust to simple inexperience.

I manage all my businesses via email and phone calls, but it doesn't mean that I don't still keep an eye on every aspect of my various organizations. I know what is happening all the time, regardless of where in the world I am. I pay employees very well, keep them motivated by giving them more than expected, and empower them. To avoid the need to micromanage, I build trust between us.

Every team, department, and business works together. If one department of a business is lacking, the results will show in the daily reports and at meetings. Solutions are created, and problems remedied. Even when you do become a successful business owner, the work doesn't stop there.

It takes a lifetime of dedication and discipline to keep a business thriving; it is easier with a dedicated team. It is easy to manage from afar when you trust your team; trust comes from the intangible benefits created when you pay more, give more, and keep more.

---

30   Ibid.

—

PERFECT MIMICKING AND MENTORSHIP

One of the greatest values of mentors is the ability to see ahead what others cannot see and to help them navigate a course to their destination.

—John C. Maxwell

No matter what industry you are in, there will always be a competitor that does many things better than you do. "Better" comes with experience.

Real estate is a very competitive market because there are multiple agents but only so many houses, and you have to convince homeowners to sell their home with you. Though it's a challenging industry to get into, it's not impossible. You have to learn to outshine your competitors, so prospective clients think of you first when they want to sell or develop a new property. The same applies to any business. Discover what will set you apart from your competitors, and make sure your company continues to thrive. To outshine your competitors, you need first to mimic their successful practices and then stand apart from them by adding on to or innovating their proven ideas and making them unique to you.

The more you know about your competitors, the better you can improve on what they offer. Always be a step ahead of them, which will give you an edge. Study their websites, marketing materials, promotions, and offers. Most importantly, study their very best people so you can one day motivate them to work for you instead. Great people and great performers don't just bring you the performance itself. I have learned how other businesses operate, their secrets, and their problems. I even discovered the very best success strategies of other organizations by learning from their best employees.

When I was new in the real estate industry, and my career as a property developer started to take shape, I did not know much about construction, architecture, or interior design. So, I studied the most admired developers in Thailand. I researched all the big players, and I slowly found out what builders, architects, and interior designers they preferred. I started to imitate them and contacted all the same builders, architects, interior designers, and graphic designers. To be the best you have to work with the best!

I remember having an intense desire to become one of the top developers soon, and I set a goal to receive an Asia Pacific Property Award within five years. It took four years and seven months until I climbed up on the stage in Bangkok to accept my first award for my very first 201-unit condominium development, which I had built and sold out. I knew from the beginning that I needed to work with the same people and companies as the very best, so I would get similar results. It worked as I imagined, and nine years later I have stood on that same stage eight different times, receiving numerous awards in all of the categories for almost all of my developments. I'm convinced that a "mimic and innovate" approach will work in any industry. If you want to be the best, learn from the very best, adapt their strategies, and then personalize those strategies.

MIMIC: THE FAST WAY TO SUCCESS

Start simple. Start small. Master the minor aspects before you try to become just like your models in only a few days. It's easy to stop, to give up. The answers are out there. Real success is available to anyone who is willing to reach out and grab it.

Mimicking others is one of my biggest secrets to success. When I want a particular type of success, or when I'm trying to finish one specific goal, I do the research and find the best people in that field, even if they are competitors. I look at what they have done, what has worked, and their principles. It's like following a scientific formula, and it is how I've risen to the top so quickly and early in my life. I've just followed the same steps that have already been taken, adapting them to my situation and needs, and have found a lifetime of success in a short time.

> *Whatever you want to be, find a person who already has achieved it, and just do it.*

BLUE HORIZON SUCCESS

I'm now best known for my property development called Blue Horizon. Blue Horizon Development Company, LTD, has been in business for more than fifteen years. We have more than 249 employees and continue to grow. In June 2017, Blue Horizon was named Top Thai Property Developer and Best New Hotel Construction and Design in the Asia Pacific Property Awards. In July 2017, Blue Horizon collected three more awards from the Thailand Property and Dot Property Group. Blue Horizon's group of portfolios includes award-winning The Beachfront, award-winning Skylight Villas, Signature Villas, and the Himalai Oceanfront Condominium. We were nominated again in 2018 as well!

It took time to reach this point, but it also took a solid team of the best employees to make it happen. I can't say that *I* created Blue Horizon; *we* did. It took a whole team of people to make this dream a reality. What started as my goal to become the best developer in Thailand turned into a dream that I now share with countless others. I've grown a company, a family of people that all work together, celebrate together, and thrive to lift each other to continued success. All it took was learning how to become the best in this industry. By studying other leaders and my competitors, I've become the best there is and have been able to bring my employees with me on this fantastic journey.

FINDING A MENTOR

One way to outshine your competitors and get the upper hand in your business is by obtaining a mentor in your industry. Mentors can come in many different forms. Earlier in this book, I mentioned my father had given me the gift of learning and education, but my mother's gift was mentoring. She was a strong woman of four amazing children, the only person who had always believed in and encouraged me to be the best I could be, to always keep chasing my dreams. Her words gave me strength. She recently lost her battle with cancer and will still be in my heart. Concerning mindset and helping me become a Law of Attraction master, authors like William Walker Atkinson, Charles Haanel, Dr. Joe Vitale, and Napoleon Hill have all been personal mentors. A mentor can be a successful coach you admire, a leader in your industry that you emulate, or a family member who always supports and motivates you no matter what.

A mentor is so beneficial because they're that person in your back pocket, your secret weapon, who will always be available to help you out. It can come from having a list of inspirational quotes from your mentor who is also an author. It can be a close friend you can always call up and ask for advice. Your mentor could have produced several motivational videos that you can access at any time. The point is, when you have quick access to a mentor, you'll always be motivated and inspired to press forward.

In a survey of its clients, MicroMentor, a mentorship consultancy, found that 83 percent of mentored businesses survived their first two years, compared to 74 percent of non-mentored companies. The same survey also found that mentored companies were more likely to launch and had greater revenue increases than those without a mentor.[31]

Mimicking the success of other businesses with a mentor is a way of fast-tracking your success.

---

31 "Impact: Business Mentoring Fuels Success," MicroMentor, accessed February 6, 2019, https://www.micromentor.org/learn-more/impact.

A mentor has also "been there, done that, and survived it!" The point of having a mentor is so that you can learn from their mistakes and their innovations. A mentor gets you to your goal faster through previous knowledge.

Though you might be able to do all the work yourself, you can't make it through this life alone. When you have someone you look up to, someone who inspires you always to strive to be the best, then you have something your competitors may not have.

This book is an excellent example of fast-tracking your success. I sought out the mentorship of Dr. Joe Vitale for my personal development and to motivate my employees. In getting to know me, Vitale started mentoring me right away. He not only had the idea that I should write a book, but showed me how I could do it. He made introductions to the right publishers and marketers and gave me the inside connections needed to make a book highly successful. He gave me book models to follow, which I did, and then I perfected the formula where I could. It takes some people years, even decades, to write the book they have inside them. I was able to do it in six months. It was due to mimicking and mentorship.

PRINCIPLE #16

—

INVEST IN YOUR EMPLOYEES

Thee lift me, and I'll lift thee. And we'll both ascend together.

—Proverb

It's not difficult hiring people, but retaining the right people is harder. You must help them grow to make sure you don't lose them.

When I started my very first company, I studied the great success masters. I read their books, watched their videos, and occasionally attended their seminars. I absorbed as much as I could from people like Napoleon Hill, Dr. Joe Vitale, Brian Tracy, Jack Canfield, and many more. I would study the chapters, write down notes and inspiring quotes, memorize them as much as I could, and, when I felt ready, conduct small courses in my own company. I would give presentations to my few employees trying to share what I had read in all these success books. I was clumsy, awkward, and unpolished, but I was relaying to them the information they had not heard before with all the passion I could muster. My passion made up for my lack of public speaking skills.

This simple act—of sharing all the knowledge I had been learning with those I also wanted to see succeed—inspired my employees. They started to ask where I had picked up all this knowledge and where they could buy the same books. Our modern world has fallen into a deep lie: most people believe that once we finish school, we stop learning, or that there is no more to discover in our fields, and we don't need to continue developing ourselves. We only start learning about ourselves and our unlimited human potential after we have graduated.

When employees have a purpose and reason to succeed, they are that much more productive at work. Employees are more dedicated, energetic, and even enthusiastic when they are striving to better themselves. That is why when I hire new employees, I always like to ask them about their goals, if only to get a better idea of them as a person. I love to hear what drives people to succeed and what new goals they are working on. When we want to achieve something particular in life, and we go after it with motivation, what we can create and accomplish often far exceeds anything we could have imagined initially.

After I listen to my employees' goals, I then ask follow-up questions to help propel them. I ask things like, "What do you think you can do this week to meet that goal?" followed with, "Okay, what about this month, next month, this year?" I like to show my employees that they can act now to fulfill those goals and that sometimes there are little goals, small things, we can accomplish throughout the next few months to obtain those big goals as well.

This same type of questioning is what I use when I need a particular report or assignment completed by a specific deadline. Instead of telling my team members that I need something done tomorrow, I will instead ask, "What do you believe that you can do to have this ready by tomorrow?" They might give me the answers right then, or they'll be honest and say that they can't get it done tomorrow, but what they can do to have it done by the following day. It creates an environment of critical thinking, of finding solutions that everyone can be a part of; this is a form of investing in employees. I take a particular interest in the way projects get completed by asking my teams how they are going to finish this or that assignment. In these scenarios, they are more honest, humble, and accountable for how they are about to take action. It builds a relationship of trust and dependency that makes each one of my businesses successful.

> *The better your team performs, the more they will achieve in life.*

FIND OUT WHAT IS IMPORTANT

My chief assistant, Nenny, has been with my organization from the very beginning. Instinctually, I knew the first time I met Nenny that she was a game-changing employee. The only problem was that she already had a job and had no interest in leaving it.

For a while, I tried to get Nenny to quit her job and come work for me by offering her higher wages and extra vacation days. She always turned me down politely. I was perplexed. Why would she not accept the position after I offered her a pay increase? Finally, I took her to dinner and spent the evening getting to know her, the things that were important to her in life, and what her fears were.

I discovered over dinner that Nenny had a daughter who didn't live in Thailand and she was afraid of not being able to provide for her daughter from afar. She was very focused on being able to have her daughter near her and oversee her daughter's education. Nenny was not interested in just making more money per hour; she cared more about how to be more involved in her daughter's life.

She was committed to her current job because she believed it posed the best future for her daughter. Nenny's motivation was centered on being with her daughter. No amount of vacation time I offered her would address the fact that she couldn't see her daughter regularly; paying her more money would not bring her closer to her daughter. She had no incentive to switch jobs, which could be risky if it didn't work out. She had security in her position; security meant she knew how to provide for her daughter. I knew that having Nenny on board would be essential in growing my company for many reasons. I decided to invest in her as an employee in a very nontraditional way. I call it an investment because I was viewing the relationship as a long-term success. I needed to contribute to that long-term success long before I would experience the results for myself.

I offered her the job because I had seen how dedicated she was to her previous employer. I knew that I wanted to gain her trust right away. I took the time to learn more about Nenny and found out the details of her daughter and their relationship. This new-found knowledge allowed me to offer Nenny a long-term agreement. I agreed that if she came to work for me and continued to be dedicated and trustworthy, I would not only fly her daughter to Thailand but I would pay for her daughter to go to an international school until she turned eighteen.

THE BENEFITS OF INVESTING IN YOUR EMPLOYEES

I've heard skeptics say that this was a risky decision. What if I flew Nenny's daughter to Thailand and put her in school and then Nenny quit? It certainly could happen. I've also heard that paying for an employee's child's education is not a good use of company money. I don't see it this way.

How many things do we as business owners invest in for the long term believing they will return big dividends?

- Advertising for new employees hoping they will be better qualified than the last employee in that position

- Advertising for new customers believing that the marketing expense will be less than the profit from new customers

- Hiring an HR manager to keep employees happy and hoping to reduce turnover

- Paying for advanced training for employees hoping they will stay longer and have better performance

- Awarding performance bonuses believing they will create better long-term productivity

- Investing in new technology hoping to increase employee output

All of these investments pose the same risk of not working out as does investing in an employee's biggest personal concerns. Investment is not without risk, so you need to make sure you value the investment itself. I believe investing in my employees is more aligned with all my wealth principles than investing in technology or infrastructure. I first and foremost invest in my employees.

Over the years, Nenny and I have formed a tight bond of trust, allowing me to rely on her during the most stressful times. I know she is looking out for the best interests of my businesses, and because of that, she has been my employee the longest.

After I hire someone and take the time to help them create their own goals, I then see what I can do to make sure they succeed; it is the first way employees recognize my investment in them. I take their goals and put them up in the office, so everyone can see who is striving to do what. I encourage my team to get to know and cheer for each other's goals. This type of communal support is another level of investment. The team members then begin to help each other succeed, and because they are driving each other's passions, my business continues to improve by leaps and bounds because my employees are happy and driven to succeed in all aspects of their lives. This deeper level of investment into your team helps employees achieve their goals, whether they are monetary, a new opportunity, or experiential. I make sure they know what I expect from them as an employee and that as a sign of how important they are to the organization I am willing to think outside the box for ways to make their outside life better—so they can be more focused and results-driven at work. It's a win-win situation that I'm quite proud of incorporating into all my businesses. Everyone is connected and progressing to achieve greatness.

PRINCIPLE #17

VALUE POSITIVITY OVER RESULTS

Great minds discuss ideas; average minds discuss events; small minds discuss people.

—**Eleanor Roosevelt**

Attracting wealth, creating new opportunities, and building a winning team have one thing in common: they are highly susceptible to the influence of negative people and thought. Negativity is like cancer. It spreads very quickly and affects everyone and everything. What does a doctor do when he finds cancer? He cuts it out very quickly before it spreads. If you want to attract great wealth into your life and build a fantastic business, then you must cut negative people out of your life, no matter how much advantage or money they bring you and your company.

IDENTIFYING THE CANCER

A few years back, one of my top sales agents—Rob, we'll call him—had his first bad month. When he stopped making sales, he began to proclaim in the office things like this:

"There are not many clients around anymore. The market is falling."

"We have too many competitors."

"I only get the bad clients with no money."

I took him into my office and allowed him to repeat all these excuses for his bad month. I reinforced to him that I understood having a bad sales month and that I was not judging him for it. I asked him to watch a few videos online by sales success experts like Brian Tracy, and I sent him articles to read, all in an attempt to get his head back in the game. I told him about my success with goal setting and visualizing. He left my office with a very noncommittal response. He was my top salesperson, and I did not want him to get discouraged, so I tried very hard to invest in him with knowledge and understanding. I mistakenly also gave him the gift of looking the other way.

Days after our meeting, he began complaining widely and openly to the other agents and marketing personnel during lunch breaks and after working hours. Things like:

"If I'm the top salesperson and I can't make a sale you know something is not right."

"The competition is getting the upper hand and taking the customers away. Things are getting worse."

It did not take long to see how Rob's cancerous influence was spreading inside my company. Within a few weeks, half of the entire sales force and half of the marketing force started to say and believe the same things. I would hear things around the office like:

"Do you think Rob is going to go work for the competition?"

"Did you see David's sales this week? How did he get a sale when Rob isn't getting any? Something is going on."

It was highly noticeable that the team's confidence, determination, and motivation were suffering. The sales results were ailing as well. Still, I worried about what would happen to revenue long-term if Rob wasn't a part of the team. Worse, if Rob left, would the other salespeople go too?

I was putting more value on results than I was on building a positive sales organization. Valuing outcomes also puts you in the position to worry, be anxious, and make rash decisions.

I had another conversation with Rob about keeping a positive outlook and stopping the negative gossip. He explained to me in the meeting that he was not responsible for the gossip. He explained that lesser salespeople gossiped out of jealousy. He also said that he was not the issue; it was the downturn in the market that was making everyone talk.

WHEN WORKPLACE CANCER IS INCURABLE

A few years back, I held a success seminar for my companies in which I invited success masters to come and speak to my team and offer a different perspective on success. One of these people was Brian Tracy, author of more than seventy books translated into dozens of languages. His popular books are *Earn What You're Really Worth*, *Eat That Frog!*, and *The Psychology of Achievement*.

I spent private time with him after the event and asked him what his best business advice was when it came to growing a company. His answer was simple: "If you know that you've already done your best to coach them, inspire them, and lead them, and they still do not improve, then don't hesitate, don't wait, let them go as quickly as possible." This method of ridding an excellent team of negative people was one of the very best pieces of advice I have ever received.

Since that day, I have adopted that strategy, and it has saved other team members and me from more cancer growth and long-term damage.

With Rob, I had no other choice than to cut the cancer out and heal the surrounding area before it spread any further. I invited him into my office a third time, and this time, I released him to find his "better fit position."

I have seen great teams and great organizations fall to the bottom due to negativity. Great teamwork erodes as negativity sets in and starts dissolving people's positive attitudes. This lack of negotiation when it comes to non-team players or negative people must hold true even if it is the top employee. When you are trying to grow your business, letting your best performer go can be very difficult and can impact sales temporarily. It shouldn't matter to you. Always value positivity over results. You can still get better results, but you can't always fix the results a non-team player or negative person has on your organization.

Even if you have a business team that consists of the very best within that industry, when you allow negativity and gossip to infiltrate that team, it will then cause them to lose even against the weakest, most inexperienced competitors. Another group will win because it is more motivated, determined, and it hasn't allowed negativity and gossip to continue.

NEGATIVITY HIDES IN COMPLACENCY

As I mentioned in a previous chapter, when selecting new employees, I take the time to get to know them and their goals, to learn what drives them and what fills their lives with passion. If they don't have any goals when I meet them, I'll help them create goals. I also try to put them on a path to achieving these goals because I know how powerful this is in creating dynamic, productive, and loyal employees. Sometimes a person is not willing to read the books I suggest or try some of the exercises I give them. Sometimes it takes a few months being with the company before I learn that people have an aversion to learning. Once I do recognize this in employees, I can deduce three things:

1. They are not team players.

2. They do not have an interest in helping others, only themselves.

3. They are not motivated to do any self-improvement. When I first say this to people, I often get pushback.

"Andres, just because they don't read the books you suggest or try the goal-setting exercises or visualization exercises you recommend, it does not mean they are not a team player."

To be clear, when I ask an employee to read a book or take part in an exercise, I am not asking them to follow my beliefs blindly. I am not asking them to give up their opinion. I am not asking them to mimic or parrot anything they read. I am asking them to be open to possibilities and new ways of thinking, because those are both crucial elements to success, both personally and as part of a team. I am asking them to try something new and see how it works for them. I am asking them to take part in a team culture, allowing me to see how open they are to the ideas of others, how much they are willing to participate in growing a great team, and how eager they are to invest in their own self-actualization.

Negative people with an aversion to learning need to be cut from your team immediately.

Not only does this ensure that negativity will not settle into your organization, but it also sets an example for the other employees. They will see you honor a culture of positivity and that it is nonnegotiable.

> *One of the most difficult things to do is separate yourself from bad conversations. However, when you do it, your life transforms overnight.*

DO NOT TOLERATE GOSSIP

It is now scientifically proven that emotions are contagious, and they spread from human to human when they are close enough to each other, like the common cold.[32] That is why I have made one of my golden rules in all my companies, organizations, and teams, even in my own family: never, ever spread gossip. Gossip fuels negativity.

If I ever end up in a negative conversation somewhere in public, I always make sure to excuse myself and pretend that I have to make an urgent phone call or go to the restroom. I refuse to get dragged down by negative energy—that leads to more problems in life and business. The same thing is true in business.

---

32 Susan Weinschenk, "Emotions Are Contagious," Psychology Today, June 1, 2016, https://www.psychologytoday.com/us/blog/brain-wise/201606/emotions-are-contagious.

GOSSIP DESTROYS TRUST AND LOWERS MORALE

If private conversations become the subject of workplace gossip, it can cause coworkers to lose trust in each other. When employees are the subject of workplace gossip, it can also negatively affect their morale. They might eventually decide to resign.

GOSSIP HINDERS TEAMWORK

When someone becomes the subject of workplace gossip, it creates a toxic working environment with a lack of unity. An employee who is too focused on the gossip may not be able to focus on work, and productivity suffers.

When you create a team of employees who focus on positively conducting themselves, encouraging other team members to think and collaborate freely, and who focus on personal development and applying it to their roles in the company and staying proactive, you will absolutely have better results in every area of your company, including workflow, productivity, loyalty, job satisfaction, growth, and revenue.

For all of these reasons, why would anyone trying to attract wealth and create opportunity in business not oppose negativity and gossip, and, more importantly, not implement strategies that help employees avoid becoming cancerous? Take these strategies, for example:

- Having a no-gossip policy

- Educating employees on positive living through books and seminars

- Goal setting

- Visualization

- Avoiding negativity

- Interacting with only positive emotions

Negativity (and the gossip that fuels it) is cancerous to a prosperous business, just as it is in personal relationships; this is why you must always value positivity over results. Making decisions based on results is not always the best choice for your relationships, business dealings, wealth attraction, or for creating unlimited opportunity. Think about it:

- If you stay in a stressful relationship because your partner has great earning potential, stress will ultimately end up breaking down the relationship. Rather than separating and remaining friends, you destroy the link in the end.

- Keeping your top salesperson despite a negative impact they have on the other team members will eventually lead to lower productivity or turnover among supporting team members. Without support, your best salesperson cannot adequately service customers. Good salespeople backed by a positive team will create more benefit in the long run than the best salesperson without team support.

- Employees who are not trained to only speak positively about your company will ultimately say the wrong things in the wrong situation, potentially impacting your profit and new opportunities.

Don't allow gossip to seep into your organization. It will breed negativity and bad energy. You need to be able to remove negative people from your business and your life in a loving way that will allow them to part without any animosity. This way, they'll still be able to feel good about themselves, and you'll feel good as well.

Surround yourself with positively driven people who will uplift you and believe in you.

Put distance between you and any negative people as quickly as possible. You always become the sum total of the people around you.

I believe so strongly that gossip is one of the biggest causes of negativity in the workplace that I am in favor of having employees sign an actual No Gossip Policy form, similar to the following one from the Pennsylvania Bar Association, so they see that I have no tolerance for it.

NO-GOSSIP POLICY[33]

Gossip drains, distracts, and decreases job satisfaction. We have all gossiped at some point, yet most of us say we don't like it. Creating a more positive and professional workplace requires a commitment to a gossip-free atmosphere.

The definition of "gossip" is a rumor or talk of a personal, sensational, or intimate nature. A gossip is someone who habitually spreads intimate or private rumors or facts.

To gossip is also a verb, which means it is something you *do*. That also means it is something you *choose* to do, and you can choose *not* to do it:

- Gossip always involves a person who is not present.

- It involves criticizing another person.

---

33 "No Gossip Policy," Pennsylvania Bar Association, accessed February 2019, https://www.pabar.org/Public/LPM/Resources/R06/Other%20Resources/No%20 Gossip%20Policy%20-%20Employee%20Handbook%20or%20Personnel%20File. pdf.

- Gossip often is about conjecture that can injure another person's credibility and reputation.

The persons signed below agree that to have a more professional, gossip-free workplace, we will:

- not speak or insinuate another person's name when that person is not present, unless it is to compliment or reference work matters.

- refuse to participate when another mentions a person who is not present in a negative light. I will change the subject or tell them I have agreed not to talk about another.

- choose not to respond to negative email or use email to spread private or derogatory information about any person in the company.

- while off the job, speak to another coworker about people at work in an unflattering light. If I have feelings, I will elect to talk to someone not in the workplace.

- use the proper channels to report to a person in authority if another person in the department does something unethical, incorrect, against procedures, or disruptive, so the authoritative party can take corrective action.

- mind my own business, do good work, be a professional adult, and expect the same from others.

LETTING NEGATIVITY GO THROUGH POSITIVITY

I have developed a way to remove these people in a way that is consistent with my Law of Vibrational Giving. Anytime I have to let someone go because of negativity or low performance, I make sure to create a personal agreement with them in the most positive way.

I take them into a private meeting room and let them know that they are not the best fit for their position. I assure them I will pay them a month's salary. This makes it less stressful since they will have some time to find another job. I make sure they have a good review and even a reference, because even though someone was not the best fit for my company, that person might excel in another. You can almost always find something positive to say about a person and should do so without reserve. I make sure they know I want them to do well. I pride myself on always being fair with anyone I work with, or anyone I meet, because I know how I treat that person is the same way others will treat me in the future.

For me to stay positive about building my team, I have to remain internally positive toward everyone and every action I take. Acknowledging that an employee is not the right fit and wishing their success in securing a new position that is a better fit can be very positive. I am releasing that person to find a company that better satisfies that particular employee. I am doing it with fairness and without creating stress. I am also removing worry from the employee by giving a recommendation and confirming I will only provide a positive reference, which allays some of the concern about having to find another job. Therefore, even if an employee is not happy about being released, I am not seen as the enemy. It is a gift, and I offer it with gratitude.

Consider the benefits you'll experience when you release employees from roles they are not suited for, release your other employees from the grasp of negativity, and free yourself from the stress of having an organization that is not running on total positivity. The benefits are numerous and all positive:

- better team morale
- better team productivity
- better results
- better leadership
- happier work environment
- happier customers
- bigger sales

PRINCIPLE #18

—

DO. BE. GO. HAVE.

You can get help from teachers, but you are going to have to learn a lot by yourself, sitting alone in a room.

—Dr. Seuss

We only get one life, and if you live it the right way, one life is more than enough. I advocate living a life of "Do. Be. Go. Have."

- *Do* the actions necessary to attract wealth and unlimited opportunity into your life.

- *Be* focused on bringing your future into reality.

- *Go* think, risk, and believe more than you feel comfortable in achieving.

- *Have* the confidence and faith that you can do it.

With year-long sunny weather, amazing food, and genuine culture, living in Phuket is precisely the life I dreamt of when I was on the streets in Stockholm. I did not get there by accident. I did what it took to get me there: plane ticket, bus ride. I became focused on building a future there: being promoted in real estate. I went farther than I ever imagined there: starting and failing in business but trying again and again. I now live there fully confident and with a specific purpose: not only to build luxury vacation developments for others, but to live in Phuket as if every day is a vacation. I spend time on Phuket's numerous sandy white beaches and sailing, exploring, and diving in the Andaman Sea. I hike the mountains of Thailand in the warm sun. When the sun sets, Phuket's renowned food scene comes alive from local street food to award-winning restaurants with amazing views. I discovered early that you don't need to travel far to live life to the fullest. It can start with you and where you are living now. However, you must "Do. Be. Go. Have."

BRINGING THE FUTURE INTO YOUR PRESENT

I had the opportunity to interview Mike Tyson, the legendary boxer and world champion. I asked him when he knew he would be a world champion. "When I was fourteen," he replied. Even before Mike Tyson won the boxing title, he naturally understood how crucial it was to experience success in the present—even if it was only in his mind. He knew as early as fourteen what being the world champion would feel like, because, in his mind, he would picture himself in the ring, defeating opponent after opponent, wearing the heavyweight champion belt, hearing the crowd cheer for him, and feeling the pride of being a world-class athlete. He imagined his achievements, trained five days a week (Do), taking any boxing match he could get

(Be), stepping into the ring with men he was afraid to fight so he could win more titles (Go), and achieved a boxing and entertainment career of full of wins, losses, criticism, and praise, with confidence and purpose (Have).

> *Don't say, "There's still time," or, "Maybe next time," because there's also, "It's too late."*

IT'S NOT ABOUT THE MONEY

Robert Kiyosaki, author of *Rich Dad Poor Dad,* asks us to "step out of the rat race."[34] I have made a habit of spending my time (and money) on excursions, holidays, travel, and team-building events with my closest friends, family, and employees. I spend the majority of my discretionary income on shared experiences. Living outside the rat race whenever possible, and bringing those closest to me along for the adventure, achieves multiple simultaneous benefits:

- I live my most passionate life.

- I inspire others to think bigger.

- I prove to those around me how much I value them.

- I become a better leader by bringing people closer.

- I improve productivity in my business by bringing back more motivated and loyal employees who are recharged and ready to succeed at even higher levels.

- I experience once-in-a-lifetime events that personally and professionally inspire me to think bigger, be more present, and attract more wealth opportunities.

---

34 Kiyosaki, op. cit.

CREATING A CULTURE OF "DO. BE. GO. HAVE."

I build a "once-in-a-lifetime" culture into every one of my companies. We engage in business that is unique; we achieve success as no other company has before, and we celebrate epically. No salary can replace this culture. The once-in-a-lifetime culture fosters loyalty; a once-in-a-lifetime job with once-in-a-lifetime benefits are both financially and experientially appealing.

Others have called us crazy when our team embarks on another adventure. We are called innovators because we have become the most productive, confident, and successful companies in Thailand. We have won numerous regional and international awards across the entire organization and continue to win them.

IN THE END "THEY WILL SAY"

Being remembered as the business owner who made billions on the beaches of Thailand is not how I want to be remembered. In the end, they will say, "Andres was a leader who created the best memories with the people in his life. He was a force for good. He contributed to making a change in the world through goodness."

This visualization is compelling for me and guides my attitude and decisions in my business and personal life. I've shared this visualization with my employees, and it has caused them to trust me at a deeper level. When I present a new idea or change direction on a project, even if they cannot yet understand why I am doing it, they trust that I am deciding in the best interest of my clients, vendors, and employees. This is especially helpful when we experience a setback or a slowdown. Rather than jump to conclusions like, "He is trying to cut corners," or, "He has ulterior motives," or, "He isn't listening to us," my teams rally around and proactively help to put things back in alignment with success. They believe in my underlying motivation, and it carries through every part of our business organization.

> *Have fun and live to work, don't work to live.*

START IMMEDIATELY DESPITE YOUR SIZE

When I give talks on business success, inevitably I hear the criticism, "Your company is big and has a lot of money. Of course you can make your employees jump out of planes. That is not practical for a new business owner, or a smaller business." I love this criticism because it allows me to demonstrate how thinking big and engaging your team has little to do with your bank account and more to do with your ability to think bigger with what you have access to.

Building a once-in-a-lifetime culture is not about how much money you have as a company, but rather the feeling you give to the company culture. Much like my feelings on vibrational giving, creating a company culture starts with the emotion you, as the business owner, attach to the elements that make up that culture.

Do encourage action in your company that brings employees together in unusual, and memorable, situations.

Be focused on the positive feelings created during any company-wide activity.

Go beyond your employees' expectations by personalizing, memorializing, and expanding on simple, everyday achievements.

Have confidence in your employees that they will engage and expand the experience to meet the needs of the company.

VOLUNTEER AS A GROUP

I love to volunteer because it is one of the best forms of vibrational giving; it is a fantastic way to get into a positive mindset, and it builds incredible team morale in the process.

Volunteering improves morale. Science has proven that doing good deeds makes you feel great. Why not help out the local community while you're at it?

Deloitte reports that the top employee engagement comes from helping employees find a common purpose in their work. It's about cultivating closer relationships through shared experiences, which are rarely expensive to implement.[35]

"We all want meaning in our lives and want to work for an organization that's contributing to the community and is socially responsible," Don MacPherson, an Aon partner who works in employee management practice, says.[36]

"When you asked [employees] to go above and beyond [on the job], they were good with doing it because they knew you were a company that cared," says Colleen Martin, a woman who managed seasonal workers for tedious jobs at an oil refinery, such as monitoring machine dials all day. To make the job "less boring" she started bringing to employees different service project opportunities. She arranged opportunities for employees to build homes on the weekends for Habitat for Humanity, send personal cards to troops in

---

35 Josh Bersin, "Becoming irresistible: A new model for employee engagement," Deloitte Insights, January 26, 2015, https://www2.deloitte.com/insights/us/en/deloitte-review/issue-16/employee-engagement-strategies.html.

36 Tamara Lytle, "7 Tips to Increase Employee Engagement Without Spending a Dime," Society for Human Resource Management, September 22, 2016, https://www.shrm.org/hr-today/news/hr-magazine/1016/pages/7-tips-to-increase-employee-engagement-without-spending-a-dime.aspx.

the Middle East, and donate to an orphanage. This is an example of employee engagement and culture curation.[37]

BE LOUD WHEN YOU GIVE RECOGNITION

It's no secret that rewards and recognition make the workplace special. At Disney, for instance, workers know that the customer experience is paramount. Disney workers report feeling very connected to their jobs and go out of their way to create unique experiences for customers. They perform better because they are recognized for their contributions as well as their group efforts. At Disney, recognition is not a small event!

Too often, though, gifts and bonuses are doled out with little fanfare. I remembered my first job as a telemarketer and how the "best people" got the rewards, and, even then, the rewards involved cash and were just handed out. There was nothing special. No once-in-a-lifetime feeling. When I read about the Yum! corporation (the parent company of Taco Bell, KFC, and other restaurant chains), I was newly inspired to create a unique work environment. The leaders there pull out kazoos, tambourines, horns, and cowbells. Each month, a different company head leads a band of employees as it marches around the building playing "music" in honor of the six or so people chosen for recognition, gathering dozens more people as they go. They create a parade in honor of the group efforts that had the most impact that month. How many times in life do we get the opportunity to have a parade in our name?

Yum! has 1.5 million corporate and franchise workers. Recognition is a company-wide priority, and local leaders figure out what that looks like for their particular location and culture. The awards

---

37   Ibid.

themselves are things you could probably pick up at a dollar store: a cape and sunglasses, an Albert Einstein bobblehead doll, and some chattering teeth. It's about the emotion behind the recognition and going out of your way to appreciate employees in ways that they would never even consider.

BE SPONTANEOUS

Who doesn't love surprises? Being spontaneous is a great way to improve the morale of employees because the simple act of being spontaneous is enough to make people happy, with the actual result being a secondary benefit. Your goal with spontaneity is to create instant happiness. Instant happiness is something that most people don't experience in life.

A surprise lunch, a movie night for the group, a surprise breakfast for the morning meeting, or even a picnic in the middle of the day can all be acts of spontaneity. If you let your people leave an hour early on a Friday, the fact that you decided to do something out of the ordinary for them goes a long way.

ENCOURAGE PAID TIME OFF

Let's face it. Even when you love what you do, you still look forward to a vacation, and you still need to take a day here and there for whatever reason. As a manager or leader, never impose guilt on employees using their earned vacation time. Give employees the time to recharge mentally, so they're full of fresh ideas upon their return.

Take Kabbage, for instance. When it comes to benefits, Kabbage is continuously working to create a comfortable and collaborative environment for team members (and their dogs!), all with an incredibly high laughter quotient. With unlimited paid time off and a six-week sabbatical program, plus in-office meditation classes and on-site courses, the benefits of working at Kabbage are numerous.[38]

Glassdoor salaried employees participate in a Vacation Matters Policy that allows employees to take vacation time when they need it without worrying about vacation accruals. Hourly employees receive up to three weeks of paid time off as well as two floating holidays and one day off each quarter to volunteer at the nonprofit of their choice.[39]

Consider an unlimited paid or flexible time off policy. Flexible days off solve the issue of finding a work-life balance for employees. Of course, it's essential to have guidelines in place, so employees don't abuse the policy, but in most cases, companies tend to see that employees take less time off than when they have a set amount of vacation time.

OFFER CONTINUOUS TRAINING

Creating a lifelong learning environment within your company helps inspire lifelong, committed employees. It's important to consider your team's career goals and work to help them obtain the education and resources they need to move toward them. Creating a culture that fosters continuous development does more than help employees build the skills they need to do their jobs.

Brad Shuck, an assistant professor at the University of Louisville in Kentucky, specializes in organizational development. He thinks

---

38 "Kabbage Benefits," Glassdoor.com, accessed February 2019, https://www. glassdoor.com/Benefits/Kabbage-US-Benefits-EI_IE606681.0,7_IL.8,10_IN1.htm.

39 Glassdoor, "Glassdoor Vacation and Paid Time Off," accessed February 2019, https://www.glassdoor.ca/Benefits/ Glassdoor-Vacation-and-Paid-Time-Off-US-BNFT29_E100431_N1.htm.

companies that invest in employee futures see higher engagement, saying, "The more the employee feels the company is investing in their future, the higher the level of engagement."[40]

One of the essential practices at Timberlane Inc. is cross-training employees. By teaching them how to perform the jobs of others, employees gain a better understanding of how each department operates. For example, office staff periodically spend time on the manufacturing floor to sand or assemble blinds.

There are many ways to encourage employees to contribute or involve themselves for little to no cost. At Timberlane, for example, employees can play Cornhole—a bean bag tossing game—during company parties, and they have an annual Thanksgiving potluck. It's caring about what you're doing and whom you're doing it with that counts.[41]

Dedicate a set portion of the team budget to education. Whether this is conferences or online training courses, the important thing is to invest in your team's education. The opportunities also build your network and establish relationships that will help employees personally, along with the business.

APPLY IT PERSONALLY AND PROFESSIONALLY

Do whatever it is you want to do in life. Be who you want to be. Go wherever you want to go. Have whatever it is you want to have right now. The key is taking the small steps now to "Do. Be. Go. Have."

Don't just think about what you want to become, how you want to succeed, and what you want to accomplish. Take action—now!

---

40 Lytle, op. cit.

41 Ibid.

As you move on from this book, may you go in peace, with the love I have for you as the reader. You have the tools; you have the knowledge. Let them fill you with excitement, with happiness, with joy. Allow yourself to see the possibilities and to know without a shadow of a doubt that anything you can imagine is possible.

Let your days fill up with small moments that work together to achieve big dreams. Every minute of every day is a blessing in some way or another, even if it comes to you first in disguise. Everything good works together for the good of all. Grasp the good around you, cling to the positive and the beneficial. Find those who are the best for you and surround yourself with those who will lift you and propel you toward success.

IN CONCLUSION

I am a high school dropout with no higher intelligence than you. I came to a country without speaking the language or understanding the culture, and with no money. If I can change my life by seizing unlimited opportunity, so can you.

If I can go from sleeping on the beaches of Thailand with a suitcase for a pillow to developing some of the most luxurious beach resorts in the world—from homeless to billionaire—then you can also turn your life into exactly what you desire.

It all starts in our minds. My message to all those who read this book is this: we live on a magical, unbelievable planet. We were born to see it, explore it, experience it, and enjoy it. Forget about the usual rat race, the same routines and habits of everyday life, and change your thinking. Get out and enjoy life! The world is yours to see and conquer. We are meant to see the magnificent wonders of this amazing heaven on earth. Unfortunately, our minds often make it into a living hell, and we get controlled by those negative thoughts. Please remember that you are not your thoughts. You are a spiritual being with the power to use your ideas to create fantastic experiences in this world.

On our deathbeds, we will not remember the money we made, or the things we bought, or the wealth we created. We will not forget our loved ones and the experiences we had on this amazing planet— the ones we saw, created, and lived. Most people think that after we pass through this life, we arrive at the promised land filled with happiness or the other place filled with condemnation. I believe that to be very wrong. We are already living in those places at this very moment. We decide how we want to live on this earth—in a state of happiness or a state of dissatisfaction.

With the power of your mind, choose happiness. Change your thinking and your actions, and you will be amazed at how beautiful life is. Being alive is the most wonderful gift to humanity. Life is short. So, don't doubt, don't second-guess, don't think that you can't do it. It's only in your mind; control it, and you will experience more than you could have ever imagined—while you are alive.

Always live life to the fullest, and everything in this world that can bring you happiness will. Just reach out and grab it, and never give up. It may have all started with a cup of coffee for me, but this book is your cup of coffee. Take it and keep going. I can't wait to hear about your success after using the 18 Principles of Wealth Attraction.

ABOUT THE AUTHORS

ANDRES PIRA

Andres Pira is a real estate development tycoon located in Phuket, Thailand. A philanthropist at heart, Pira lives by the Buddhist virtue of giving. Over the past decade, he gratefully celebrated his business successes by giving back to society. His company Phuket Condos & Homes has for years been involved with Phuket Has Been Good to Us, established after the 2004 tsunami to improve the economic and life chances of young people. Pira's philosophy is, "A man's true wealth is the good he does in this world."

Making the most out of his life, Pira spends his spare time traveling the world, learning new cultures, and exploring unbound territories. At the age of thirty, he became immersed in the adrenaline of extreme sports. He enjoys mountain climbing, skydiving, bungee jumping, skiing, bodybuilding, and football. "The adrenaline and stress of an adventure are better than a thousand peaceful days" is often heard from the man in action.

Andres Pira and his group of companies are worth approximately 1.8 Billion THB. A serial businessman, he has expanded investments to include a gym, law office, a gas station, several coffee shops, and more.

DR. JOE VITALE

Dr. Joe Vitale, once homeless but now a motivating inspirator, known to his millions of fans as "Mr. Fire!" is the globally famous author of numerous best-selling books, such as *The Miracle, The Attractor Factor, Zero Limits, Life's Missing Instruction Manual, The Secret Prayer, The Awakened Millionaire*, and *Attract Money Now.*

Vitale starred in the blockbuster movie *The Secret*, as well as a dozen other films. He has recorded many best-selling audio programs, from *The Missing Secret* to *The Zero Point*. He is also a self-help singer-songwriter, with fifteen albums out and many of his songs nominated for the Posi Award (considered the Grammy awards of positive music).

Vitale created Miracles Coaching®, The Awakening Course, The Secret Mirror, Hypnotic Writing, The Awakened Millionaire Academy, and many more life-transforming products. He lives outside of Austin, Texas, with his pets.

INDEX